Student Workbook

Writing and Reporting News
A Coaching Method

SEVENTH EDITION

Carole Rich

Prepared by

Carole Rich

 WADSWORTH
CENGAGE Learning™

Australia • Brazil • Japan • Korea • Mexico • Singapore • Spain • United Kingdom • United States

WADSWORTH
CENGAGE Learning

For product information and technology assistance, contact us at **Cengage Learning Customer & Sales Support, 1-800-354-9706**

For permission to use material from this text or product, submit all requests online at **www.cengage.com/permissions** Further permissions questions can be emailed to **permissionrequest@cengage.com**

ISBN-13: 978-0-8400-2938-6
ISBN-10: 0-8400-2938-1

Wadsworth
20 Channel Center Street
Boston, MA 02210
USA

Cengage Learning is a leading provider of customized learning solutions with office locations around the globe, including Singapore, the United Kingdom, Australia, Mexico, Brazil, and Japan. Locate your local office at: **www.cengage.com/global**

Cengage Learning products are represented in Canada by Nelson Education, Ltd.

To learn more about Wadsworth, visit **www.cengage.com/wadsworth**

Purchase any of our products at your local college store or at our preferred online store **www.cengagebrain.com**

Printed in the United States of America
1 2 3 4 5 6 7 15 14 13 12 11

Table of Contents

Changing Concepts of News   1

The basic qualities in news stories involve conflict, timeliness, proximity, unusual nature, human interest and news about celebrities. Those concepts are still the same in online publications, but other concepts of news are changing. These exercises are intended to help you understand some of the basic qualities of news and the changing values of news.

1-1. Qualities of news

Some of the main qualities of newsworthiness are timeliness, proximity (news in or near your community), unusual nature, prominence (stories about celebrities or prominent people), human interest and conflict. Other newsworthy angles include entertainment, helpfulness (such as consumer news), and trends (stories that show patterns in society). Using these qualities as your guide, identify the newsworthy elements in the following items; some items may have several qualities:

a. Ninety-eight alligators were found in the bedroom of a man who lives in Omaha, Neb.
News qualities:

b. The campus security office has released crime statistics for the first six months of the semester.
News qualities:

c. Relatively inexpensive medical treatment, such an increasing supply of cheap vaccines and antibiotics, could help save more than half of the 3 million infants who die each year, a new study has found.
News qualities:

d. Residents in your community disagree with plans to change school boundaries, forcing nearly 500 of 7,000 children to change schools next year. Members of the public will express their viewpoints at a public hearing tonight.
News qualities:

e. Oprah Winfrey was named one of the richest women in America in the annual *Forbes* magazine ratings. Her production company generates about 40 percent of its revenue from the talk show.

News qualities: _____

f. A man in your town was gardening, but he didn't dig up weeds. He dug up his gold wedding band that he had lost 30 years ago.

News qualities: _____

g. The average age of college students is increasing. One out of four college students is over age 30.

News qualities: _____

1-2. Analyze online versions of print and broadcast news

Write a few paragraphs to answer the following questions and discuss your answers in class.

If your local paper, radio station or broadcast news outlet is online, compare the online version to the print or broadcast version as follows:

1. What qualities of the online version differ from the print one?
2. What qualities of the online version differ from the broadcast one?
3. Are there any qualities of the site that would entice you to read the news online instead of in print or broadcast?

1-3. Hard-news and feature stories

Write brief paragraphs to answer the following items and discuss your answers in class.

a. Using your community or campus newspaper, identify three hard-news stories and three feature stories.

b. Using a website for a newspaper or broadcast news station, identify three hard-news stories and three feature stories.

c. Compare the qualities of news in the hard-news stories and the features. How do they differ?

The Basic News Story   **2**

2-1. Crime Story

Read the following information and write a focus sentence at the top of your story. Then jot down an order for your story. Assume that you are a reporter in Tampa, Fla., and you are writing this story for the Monday morning newspaper. Ethical discussion: This information includes the race of the suspected robbers, and racial identification has become a controversial issue. Would you include race in the story? Why or why not?

Location: Riverview section of Tampa.

Facts: This information comes from Tampa sheriff's deputies: Two robbers burst into a home in Riverview at 11:30 p.m. Sunday. The home was owned by Grace Ford, 20. Ford was sitting in a front room with her baby, Brandi, 10 months old, who was in a playpen. Ford's sister, Cynthia, 16, also was in the room.

According to sheriff's reports: Both men were described as white, from 18 to 20 years old and of medium height and weight. One man was wearing a ski mask and jogging pants with the letters "UF" (for University of Florida) on the side. The other wore a white shirt and a baseball cap. Neighbors heard shots and called the sheriff's deputies. The men got away in a car that had been waiting in a nearby cemetery.

[The following information comes from an interview with Grace Ford.]

She said the robbers pushed her, her baby and her sister from room to room. They took about $5,000 worth of jewelry. The dog, a Rottweiler named Elka, began barking. The robbers fired three shots at the dog. They missed. The baby began crying. Ford said she picked her up and found a bullet hole in Brandi's diaper with the bullet imbedded in the diaper. Direct quotes from Ford: "There was about an inch left to the diaper that it didn't pierce. They were extra thick."

Based on a story from the *St. Petersburg* (Fla.) *Times.* Used with permission.

2-2. Find the focus

Read the following information and ask yourself what is the most important or interesting fact. Write a focus sentence identifying that newsworthy angle:

a. *The New England Journal of Medicine* released a study today. The study says people who abruptly quit drinking coffee may suffer effects of caffeine withdrawal. Some of the symptoms include headaches, depression, anxiety and fatigue. The study says that even people who drink fewer than three cups of coffee a day may be affected.

b. A new law went into effect yesterday in Maine. The law affects all businesses that have more than 25 employees. The law requires employers to hire one physically challenged worker for every 25 employees. Under the law, employers must post advertisements seeking individuals with physical challenges as defined under the Americans with Disabilities Act.

c. A professor from another college is scheduled to speak on your campus. The speaker has written that those who attacked the World Trade Center on Sept. 11, 2001, were justified in their actions because of previous U.S. abuses. Alumni have asked that the speech be canceled.

d. Police suspected two men of drug dealing. Police witnessed the men exchanging money and what appeared to be heroin. But after they arrested the men, police couldn't find the heroin. Police called in their drug-sniffing dog. The dog headed directly to one man's sneakers. Inside the sneakers was a pound of heroin. The two men were charged with drug trafficking.

e. A man in your community received a postcard yesterday from his father, who lived in a nearby town and had just returned from a trip. "Please come over so your mother and I can show you pictures of our trip," the postcard said. "I guess my father wondered why I never came over," said the son, Jason Gott. His father and mother died several years ago. The postcard that arrived yesterday was sent 30 years ago.

2-3. Fire

Write a news story based on the following information. Decide what material needs to be attributed. Use yesterday as your time frame, but write the day of the week, which is the preferred Associated Press style. Use a new paragraph for each new thought and a new paragraph for the start of a quotation.

This information comes from Lynn Wilbur, University Place assistant fire chief:
A fire occurred in a Tacoma suburb called University Place in Washington. Wilbur said the fire started in a corner unit at the Meadow Park Garden Court apartments. It spread to a two-bedroom apartment next door through a common attic the two apartments shared. Both apartment units were destroyed, and two others were damaged. Four families were left homeless. About 12 people had to be relocated. It was a two-alarm fire (which means two fire companies responded to the fire). Investigators have not confirmed the cause of the fire. The fire may have been started by a stove that was left on in one unit. "The pots were melted down on it." No one was injured. A pet cat died in the fire.

Information from apartment manager Steve Edwards:
He said he couldn't relocate the families in the apartment complex because it was filled to capacity. He said some residents may have to seek shelter with the American Red Cross.
(continued)

4

'Information from Rosemary Hurlburt, who lived in one of the apartments: Her apartment was gutted. She said she and her two daughters were at a convenience store when the fire started. She said she lost a lot of new possessions. "We just got new stuff," Hurlburt said. "My 5-year-old daughter just had a birthday party. We just got her a brand-new bunk bed set."

Based on a story from *The Oregonian.* Used with permission.

2-4. Program advance

Instructions: A program about date rape will be offered at your school tonight. Your editor hands you a press release and tells you to write a story about the upcoming program. This type of story is called an advance. You interview one of the panelists who will be on the program, and you get comments from people sponsoring the event. Instead of writing a lead announcing the program, try writing a lead based on something one of your sources tells you. Ask yourself what you find most important or interesting, and use that in your lead. Then write a nut graph giving the basic information about what, where, when and so forth. You do not need to use all the quotes. Here are your notes:

Notes from a press release: There will be a forum tonight about date rape. The program is called "Date Rape, Acquaintance Rape." It is sponsored by the Emily Taylor Women's Resource Center. The program will be held in the Pine Room of the Student Union on your campus. It will be conducted from 7 p.m. to 9 p.m. It is open to men and women. The forum will feature a film, "Campus Rape." Panelists will discuss issues in the film and an audience-participation discussion will follow.

Notes from interview with Sherill Robinson, graduate assistant in the Resource Center: She said the forum would address problems that contribute to date rape, such as miscommunication, drugs and alcohol. "Regardless of those things, unless a woman says 'yes,' it's rape," she said. She said she hoped people would become aware of what date rape was. She shows you an advertisement for the forum that defines date rape as forced sexual intercourse by someone you know.

Notes from interview with Barbara Ballard, director of the Resource Center: She said the center sponsored an outreach program, which brought sexual assault programs to residence halls, scholarship halls and fraternities. "When I came here there was no such thing as date rape or acquaintance rape," she said. "Those things didn't even have a title. Now it's a topic that's discussed, and people are a lot more educated about it."

Notes from interview with Sharon Danoff-Berg, a graduate assistant in the Emily Taylor Resource Center: At least one in four women will be sexually assaulted in their lifetime. About 90 percent of college rape victims are violated by someone they know. She says that is why she agreed to be one of four student panelists on the program. "There's this myth that most rapes are stranger rapes, where someone attacks you from out of the dark. That does happen, but not in

5

the majority of rapes. People need to understand it's not the fault of the woman. Nobody deserves to be sexually assaulted or does anything to ask for it. The rapist is the one who needs to be held accountable."

2-5. Burglary

Instructions: Write a news story based on the following information. Write a focus sentence on top of the story. You are a reporter for a Louisville newspaper, and you interviewed this man after you read the report of the burglary in the police records. Be careful to attribute any material that you cannot substantiate as factual. You do not have to use the quotes in one block. Use them where you think they fit best. Your time frame is yesterday (but use the day of the week).

Information comes from Roy L. Jones, 60: He was having lunch with a friend at a Shoney's restaurant, 811 Eastern Parkway in Louisville. He parked his 1990 Oldsmobile in the restaurant parking lot. Inside the car he had a package wrapped in a plastic bag on the floor. When he returned to his car about 30 minutes after he entered the restaurant, the package was gone. The back door was open, and the glove compartment had been rifled. Inside the package was an $8,000 artificial leg. He had gone to Falls City Limb and Brace Co. before lunch to have his hip-to-floor prosthesis adjusted. He reported it to the police yesterday, but the leg has not turned up. He had locked the car, but the thief broke into it.

"I'm disgusted as hell, is all I can say. I bet whoever took it, when they opened the package is as disappointed as I am. I just hate to go through all the hassle of getting another one made. You have to go down there for a fitting, and then you have to go down there again."

He said the leg is probably covered by insurance but that doesn't make him feel any better. He lost his left leg more than 30 years ago in an industrial accident. He uses a wheelchair when he goes out. He uses the artificial leg to move around his house. He had another one, but it no longer fit. He needed further amputation two years ago. That's why he needed the new leg. He lives at 950 Samuel St. in Germantown.

Information from Louisville police Sgt. Frank Lavender: No one has been arrested. The item that was stolen has not been found. He said that this misfortune reinforces a point that police have been trying to convey to citizens: It's not enough just to lock your car. "We're trying to encourage people to look into their cars and see what's in there and put it in the trunk. People need to be more careful."

6

Convergent and Mobile Media 3

3-1. Multimedia site critique

Critique any two multimedia sites that you choose for any or all of these multimedia journalism elements: polls, chats, podcasts, blogs, audio, video interactive features. Write the name of the site, the URL and a brief critique (about a page). You might start with winners of the Online News Association (*http://journalists.org*) and click on the Online Journalism Awards link on the left menu.

3-2. Convergent media site critique

In a news organization that is truly convergent, news is posted first on the Web and updated throughout the day. A news story will also be broadcast and published in print for the newspaper. TBO.com, the site for the *Tampa Tribune* and its broadcast partner, WFLA *(http://www.wfla.com)* is one example of a convergent media operation. If your local news print publication has a partner broadcast station, you can compare how a story is presented in print and broadcast and online. If you don't have a local site, try the *Tampa Tribune* site and its partner broadcast station WFLA. Go to TBO.com and choose a story to compare first in the *Tampa Tribune* site and then click on the link for WFLA News Channel on Your side. Write a brief critique of how one news story is presented both media. Discuss the differences in leads on the stories, updated material, use of video (if available) and interactive features such as blogs, posted comments, polls or questions. On your critique, write the name of the story, the URL and your comments including a list of convergent media features.

3-3. News story for print, broadcast and Web convergent media

a. You are a reporter for the local newspaper and you are listening to the police radio when you hear a 911 call about a fire. You call the fire department and officials give you a brief report about the fire. TV crews from your partner broadcast station are on their way to the fire to get video. Before you head to the scene, you file a brief breaking news report for your website. This is all the information you have from the fire department dispatcher at the moment. Rewrite it in news story form for the Web.

Shortly before 3:00 PM today, 18 units of the (your town) Fire Department responded to a reported structure fire at 6112 Prosperity Drive in the east part of town. Several calls were made to 911, including one from a resident who was trapped on the third floor of the home. First arriving units from Station 6 reported light smoke showing from the second floor of the three story structure. Firefighters located the trapped occupant and carried her to safety outside. Another occupant was trapped inside. The person's condition is not known at this time. The cause of the fire is currently under investigation.

b. You are preparing your story for the 5 p.m. news broadcast. At this point you have a little more information. Write the story for broadcast using present tense and active voice. Here is the additional information:

Crews from Engine 14 and Truck 3 entered the home and began to extinguish the fire on the second floor and quickly proceeded to the third floor where they located the trapped occupant and carried her to safety outside. While extinguishing the fire and continuing the search on the second floor, crews from Engine 3 discovered another occupant and carried him to safety. Paramedics from Stations 3 and 6 treated and then transported the two patients to the hospital where they are undergoing treatment for smoke inhalation. Three additional family members reside in the structure and were not home at the time of the fire. The Alaska Chapter of the American Red Cross is providing assistance to the five displaced family members.

c. You now have to write your story for the newspaper, which will not be published until the next day. You have posted as much information as possible with updates on your Web site. You've interviewed the fire chief and you have some new information about the origin, but the cause is still under investigation. How will you give the story a fresh approach? Here is some additional information from fire officials:

The fire originated in the kitchen, located on the second floor. The cause of the fire is currently under investigation. Firefighters reported smoke detectors were sounding on the third floor of the home only. Residents are reminded that smoke detectors give you and your family time to escape in the earliest stages of a fire when there still is time to evacuate safely. The man and woman who were taken to the hospital were both in their 60s where they are being treated for smoke inhalation. Their names and conditions were not available before you went to press. Capt. Bob Fireproof said the house in the 6000 block did not have interior doors, which might have helped save the woman who died. "If there was a door, the lady could have closed the bedroom door and been fine," he said. The fire completely destroyed the three-story house but an estimate of the damage has not been determined. Fire officials suspect unattended cooking, but that has not been officially determined.

3-4. Mobile media rewrite

Access a news story from the Web on your cell phone. Rewrite it for mobile media.

Social Media 4

4-1. Blogs for reporting

Choose a beat that you would like to cover such as sports, politics, family issues, environment or other subject and find at least five blog sites that you would access regularly for information about your beat. Write the name of the blog site and the link. For example, you might start with Google and search blogs related to your topic.

4-2. Social networking survey

Conduct a survey of your classmates and other students in your school to determine which social networking sites they use and for what purpose. Discuss your results in class. Include the following questions:

On which of these sites do you have an account?
Facebook
Flickr
LinkedIn
MySpace
YouTube
Other or none of these

What is your main purpose in using these sites?
To communicate with friends or family
To be informed about topics of interest to me
To meet people with like interests
To find people to date
Other: Please specify

How much time do you spend each week on social networking sites?
Less than one hour
One to two hours
Three to four hours
Five hours or more

4-3. Twitter and Facebook reporting

Using any major news story for the day, check Twitter and Facebook for sources and leads you would follow if you were reporting on that story. Write a brief critique about the information you are finding. Is the information credible? What information would you want to use? What are the pros and cons of using Twitter for breaking news?

4-4. Social media source list

Choose a beat that you would like to cover for your campus news media. Using Twitter, Facebook, LinkedIn and other social media, build a source list by including people you would like to follow and sites you would check regularly. For example, if you had a health beat, you might follow the Centers for Disease Control on Twitter and Facebook.

4-5. Converting leads into tweets

Using your local or campus newspaper or website, convert the leads of five stories into tweets (140 characters including punctuation and links). Would your tweets entice readers to click into the full story linked to your post?

4-6. Social media for story ideas

What are some of the main interests of college students on social media sites? Scan Twitter, Facebook and other social media sites to get story ideas. Write a list of at least five ideas for news or feature stories you could develop for your campus or local news media.

4-7. Social media terminology

Create a quiz of 10 new terms that social media has created. Exchange your quizzes with a classmate or test your journalism class. How many new terms did you learn from your own quiz or that of your classmates? Make a list of new terms and websites that you think are helpful.

4-8. Write a blog and Twitter post

Choosing a topic that would be of interest to your friends or people in your community, write a blog using the tips in your textbook. Underline keywords that a search engine might find. Then write a tweet to promote your blog.

Sources and Online Research

5

5-1. Online Scavenger Hunt #1 – Government resources

Instructions: Find the sources in these questions and write the answers on a separate document or using the forms below. Include the name of the site and the URL. To keep these instructions, either print this page or copy and paste it into a Word document as follows:

- Pull down the edit menu and select all. Then hit copy. Open a Word document and pull down the Edit menu to paste.
- To save time writing URLs, keep your browser and Word documents open. When you find the site you want, highlight the address in the browser bar. Pull down the Edit menu to copy; then switch to your Word document and pull down the Edit menu to paste.

Question 1: Weather Story #1

You are writing a weather story about a hurricane, and you want to put it in perspective. Find a site that offers a list of hurricanes, and write the name of the site and the URL; then answer these questions: Clue: Check the National Hurricane Center.

a. Name the costliest hurricane in the United States since 1900.

b. When and where did it occur?
c. How much were the damages?

Question 2: Weather Story #2

You are writing a story about earthquakes. Find a site that offers good tips on earthquake preparedness. Clue: Check the U.S. Geological Survey. Write the URL for the site.

Question 3: Plane Crashes

A small plane has crashed in or near your community. You want to find out how many plane crashes with fatalities occurred in your community and/or your state in the past year. Clue: Check the National Transportation Safety Board under aviation and do a query for your state or area in the past year or two.

a. How many fatal crashes occurred in the last year?

b. How many nonfatal crashes occurred in the last year?

c. If the type of plane or company involved has had more than one fatal crash in the last year or two, check the record of that company using the same query site.

d. In 2000 the NTSB conducted a major investigation of an airplane crash in which 88 people died. What was the airline?

11

Question 4: U.S. Census Statistics

You are writing a story about population growth in your state. The U.S. Census Bureau predicts that in the foreign-born population of the United States will grow significantly. In 2010, the Census Bureau reported that more than half of the growth of the total population in the United States was due to the increase in the Hispanic population, which grew by 43 percent. Using the most recent census, localize this story:

Clue: U.S. Census Bureau – people – projections for your state.

a. What is the total population for your state based on the most recent census statistics available?

b. What was the increase in the Asian population in the U.S. from 2000 to 2010?

c. What racial group had the largest increase in your state from 2000 to 2010?

Question 5: Crime Story #1

You are writing a story about sex offenders in areas around colleges.

a. Find a site that lists sex offender registries in the U.S. What is the URL?

b. Check the sex offender registry in your state and identify any offenders in your area.

c. Check the Maryland sex offender registry and click on the interactive map to find registered sex offenders near colleges in Maryland. What is the URL? What type of information is available?

Question 6: Crime Story #2

You are writing a story about campus crime. You want to compare your college crime statistics with those of others in your state or universities of comparable size. Find a government site that offers more than 6,000 college and university crime statistics. Clue: Search the U.S. Dept. of Education's Office of Postsecondary Education for campus security statistics. You can also check an organization called Security on Campus.

a. Check the police statistics on your own university's website (if they are listed) and compare them with the ones listed on the education site.

b. How many forcible sex offenses were reported on your campus (from the latest year available)? How many burglaries?

Question 7: Political Reporting #1

You are writing a story about campaign contributions to senators in your state. Find a site that will give you that information. Clue: Check the Federal Election Commission or Opensecrets.org.

a. What are the latest totals for money your two senators received?

Question 8: Political Reporting #2

You are checking contributions on a state level. Clue: Check followthemoney.org

a. How much money did your governor receive in campaign contributions in his or her last campaign?

b. What was the total amount of contributions the governor received in the last election?

c. What is the limit on the amount of money for personal contributions to a campaign in your state?

Question 9: Government Statistics #1

You want quick access to government statistics for a variety of federal agencies. Find a site that will link you to them. Clue: fedstats

a. Find the latest government figures for tuition costs of college and universities. (Check under fast facts for education).

a. What was the average tuition, fees, room and board at four-year public institutions for the latest year available?

b. What was the average tuition, fees, room and board at four-year private colleges and universities?

Question 10: Government Statistics #2

Find the home page for your state. a. Write the URL.

5-2. Online Scavenger Hunt #2 – Personal and professional research

Instructions: Find the sources in these questions and write the answers or email them to your instructor using the form below; include the name of the site and the URL (Web address). To keep these instructions, print this page or copy and paste it into a Word document as follows:

- Pull down the Edit menu to Select All. Then hit copy. Open a new Word document and pull down the Edit menu to paste.
- To save time writing URLs, keep your browser and Word documents open. When you find the site you want, highlight the address in the browser bar. Pull down the Edit menu to copy. Then switch to your Word document and pull down the Edit menu to paste.

Question 1: International Information #1

You are planning to travel abroad, and you want to check the safety of the country you are visiting. Clue: The U.S. Department of State issues warnings for U.S. travelers.

a. You are hoping to go to Haiti. What warning or advice does the State Department give U.S. travelers?

b. You're planning a trip to Mexico. What should you know about weapons violations?

Question 2: More International Information #2

On your trip, you need to know how much money your dollar is worth in foreign currency.

a. Find a site that will convert dollars into the currency of the country you are visiting. Clue: Try a universal currency converter.

b. How many French francs can you get for $100 in U.S. dollars?

c. How many Mexican pesos will your $10 be worth?

Question 3: International Information #3

You have to reach a source in London, and you want to know the time difference so you don't call in the middle of the night. Find a site that will give you time around the world. Clue: Search for an international time clock.

13

Question 4: Background Research #1

You are assigned to interview Tom French, a Pulitzer-Prize winning journalist who is coming to your school to talk about feature writing. You need to do background research in a hurry. You are not even sure what newspaper he works for. You only know that he won the Pulitzer for feature writing in1998.

a. How will you find a quick biography of him and his prize-winning stories? Clue: Check the Pulitzer site. You might also check amazon.com to see if he has written any books.

b. What is the name of his prize-winning series?

c. What books has he written?

Question 5: Background Research #2

You are writing a concert review and you want to use the quote: "If music be the food of love, play on." You are not sure where the quote originated. How can you quickly check the source? Clue: Check Bartlett's quotations.

a. What is the name of the play from which this quote is taken?

b. Who wrote the play?

Question 6: Job-related sites

All media organizations have sites with tips and information for students and professionals in their fields.

a. Find an organization geared to public relations practitioners, and write the name and URL of the site.

b. Find an organization geared to professionals in radio and television and write the name and URL.

c. Find a list of internships geared to students entering newspaper careers on a site for the American Society of Newspaper Editors. Write the Web address.

Question 8 – Environmental beat information

You have the environmental beat and you are writing a story about hazardous wastes in your community. Find resources from the Society of Environmental Journalists. Write the URL of the SEJ site.

Question 9 - Diseases

You are writing a story about sexually transmitted diseases among college students for your campus newspaper. You have heard that Chlamydia is the fastest growing disease in this age group. Find a reliable government source for information and answer these questions:

a. Name the government source and URL. Centers for Disease Control and Prevention: *http://www.cdc.gov/std/chlamydia/default.htm*

b. What is Chlamydia?

Question 10 – Cost of living

You currently attend the University of Florida, and you live in Gainesville, Fla., but you have been offered a salary of $45,000 for a public relations job in New York City. It sounds like a good deal for an entry-level job, but can you afford it? What is the difference in the cost of living between New York and Gainesville? Check a cost of living salary calculator and write the percent of difference in the cost of living.

14

5-3. Website credibility

List five factors you should consider to check the credibility of websites;

1. _____

2. _____

3. _____

4. _____

5. _____

5-4. Sources terminology

Define the following terms:

a. On the record _____

b. Off the record _____

c. Background _____

d. Deep background _____

15

Interviewing Techniques 6

6-1. Classmate interview – note taking:

Pair up with a classmate and conduct a brief interview about any subject of interest to you or any controversy on campus. For example, you could ask your classmate's opinion about grades, requirements for your major, music preferences, experiences students had in study-abroad programs (if applicable), concerns about graduation or getting a job, and so forth. The point is to get as many good direct quotes as you can. Also take notes on basic information – the person's hometown, birth date and other biographical data – so you can test your recall. Just do this very briefly, about five or 10 minutes. Read back what direct quotes you have taken, and ask the student if that sounds accurate. Then switch roles. If you prefer, tape record your interviews and check the accuracy of your notes when you replay the tape.

6-2. Your listening profile

Do you struggle writing full quotes in your notes when you interview sources? Are you thinking of what you will say rather than listening to what the source says? If so, you probably need to improve your listening skills. The prerequisite for taking good notes is good listening. This is an unscientific test. It is meant only to help you identify your strengths and weaknesses in listening skills. Rate yourself for your listening skills by circling the answer
that best describes you.

a. On a scale of 1 to 10 (1= terrible to 10 = excellent) rate yourself as a listener.

>   1   2   3   4   5   6   7   8   9   10

b. On a scale of 1 to 10, (1= terrible to 10 = excellent) how do you think your friends would you rate you as a listener?

>   1   2   3   4   5   6   7   8   9   10

c. When you are talking with friends, do you interrupt?

>   Often   Sometimes   Rarely   Never

16

d. When you receive instructions verbally in a class, how often do you need to have them repeated so you understand them?

Often   Sometimes   Rarely   Never

e. When you listen to your favorite songs with words, how often do you know the score by heart?

Often   Sometimes   Rarely   Never

f. When you are in your lecture classes, what factors inhibit your listening skills?
   (1) Boredom
   (2) Thoughts of personal problems
   (3) Difficulty hearing
   (4) Lack of interest in the subject matter
   (5) Limited attention span
   (6) Other
   (7) None of the above

g. When you are talking with your friends, what factors inhibit your listening skills?
   (1) Boredom
   (2) Thoughts of personal problems
   (3) Difficulty hearing
   (4) Lack of interest in the subject matter
   (5) Limited attention span
   (6) Other
   (7) None of the above

h. When you are interviewing a source for a story, what factors inhibit your listening skills?
   (1) Boredom
   (2) Thoughts of personal problems
   (3) Difficulty hearing
   (4) Lack of interest in the subject matter
   (5) Limited attention span
   (6) Other
   (7) None of the above

i. When you are interviewing a source for a story, how often do you concentrate more on what you are going to ask next instead of what the source is saying?

Often   Sometimes   Rarely   Never

j. Now look at the answers you have circled. Do you notice any patterns? Are you thinking about personal problems or questions you might ask when you are conversing with friends or sources? Is your major problem a limited attention span, indicating lack of concentration or boredom? Using these answers as a guide or others that characterize your listening habits, identify your weaknesses:

I need to work on improving my listening skills by overcoming:

_____	_____
_____	_____
_____	_____
_____	

6-3. Peer Coaching

Pair up with a classmate and take turns coaching each other on a story you are planning to use for a class assignment. Coach each other on the idea and on other phases of the story. If you are coaching before the interview has been conducted, brainstorm some questions with your partner. If you are coaching after the interview, use the suggested questions for writing guidance. Your role as the coach is to ask guiding questions and to listen to your partner's answers. If you don't have someone to coach you, try to answer these questions yourself before you do your interview. Here are some coaching questions, but you may add more:

Coaching on the idea:
1. What is the story about? Answer in one or two sentences.
2. What is the focus?
3. What's the point – the "so-what" factor?
4. Why are you writing about this now? Is there a timeliness factor?
5. What's new, unusual, different, helpful or indicative of a pattern/trend in this story?
6. If this idea is for a feature about some previous event, what makes it newsworthy now?
7. What effect, if any, will this story have on readers?
8. Why would readers want to be informed about this topic?
9. What strikes you as interesting about this topic?

Coaching for the interview:
1. What are the main points the reader needs to know to understand this issue?
2. Do you have sources to confirm, react or provide other points of view? What sources should you contact?
3. Do you have background about the person or issue? Is there any previous related story you should check?
4. What do you want to know? (The coach can add some questions here.)

18

5. What difficulties are you anticipating? Do you have any alternative ways of getting this information?

Writing the questions:

The best quotes happen when you ask questions that begin with words such as "how", "why", "describe" and "discuss".

1. Questions that begin with "is" and "are" often may end with yes or no answers.

2. Write your questions in order.

3. Make certain you ask the most important question even though it may take several times to get an answer.

Coaching after the interview:

1. What struck you as most interesting in the interview? Was it related to the focus?

2. Do you have enough information to back up your focus? If not, should you change your focus?

3. What interesting anecdotes or facts did you learn from the interview?

6-4. Dissect a newspaper or broadcast story

Read a newspaper story or tape a TV story and dissect it by writing the questions you think the reporter asked to get the information or sound bites. Then discuss or write additional questions you think the reporter should have asked.

6-5. Police story

The police department has issued this news release, and you are interviewing the police chief or the police spokesman about this crime. Write at least five questions that you would ask. Substitute the name of your local police department for this story. Write a brief story from the information you have and any additional information you acquire from interviews. (Your instructor or another student may play the roles of a police spokesman or other people you decide to interview.)

Detectives are seeking the identity and location of a suspect believed responsible for two recent robberies. The suspect in both cases is described as a white male in his mid to late 20's who is approximately 5'6 to 5'9" tall. The male is further described as being clean shaven and in at least one instance was not wearing eyeglasses. The male was wearing jeans pants, a stocking type hat and a medium to dark colored ski-type winter jacket.

The most recent robbery occurred at about 1:40 AM this morning (use today's day of the week) at the 700 block of West Main Street. Patrol officers responded to the Tesoro station after the victim called 911, reporting that he had been stabbed by an unknown assailant.

The victim reported that the male suspect had entered the store and began demanding money. When the victim attempted to physically push the suspect from the store, the male began

19

punching at the victim's torso area. After the suspect ran from the location, the victim determined that he had been stabbed multiple times.

Fire Department Paramedics responded to the scene and transported the victim to a local emergency room for treatment.

The earlier robbery occurred on Tuesday evening at about 11:30 p.m. The robbery occurred to a Tesoro station located at the 1200 block of Parkside Road. During this robbery, the female clerk described a suspect similar in description from this morning's incident. The male brandished a large knife and demanded money from the clerk.

6-6. Holocaust speaker

A well-known Holocaust survivor is scheduled to speak at your campus. Your university has issued a brief news release, but you need to gather more information for an interview with the speaker. Check the Web for background research and write a more complete news release or a brief story for your campus newspaper. Make sure you do attribute information you take from the Web. Write at least five questions you would ask Mrs. Klein and add at least five facts you would include in the story based on your online research.

Holocaust survivor Gerda Weissmann Klein, who married one of the GIs who liberated her and her fellow prisoners in 1945, will visit (use your campus) late this month for three appearances. Gerda Weissman was 15 and living in Bielsko, Poland, in 1939 when German troops invaded, starting World War II. She and her family suffered through the occupation, living for a time in a ghetto. In 1942 the Nazis sent her parents to the death camp at Auschwitz. It was the last time Gerda would see them.

She then suffered through a succession of slave-labor camps, followed by a 350-mile forced march toward the end of the war. Of the 2,000 women marchers who endured exposure, starvation and arbitrary execution, only Klein (then Weissmann) and some 120 others survived. She weighed 68 pounds when they were found at the German-Czech border by Kurt Klein and others in the 5th Infantry Division on May 7, the day before Germany's official surrender.

Gerda Klein's autobiography, "All But My Life," in print for 50 years and 60 editions, was the basis of the 1995 HBO film, "One Survivor Remembers," winner of the Academy Award for short documentary. She has written several other books. She lives in Arizona.

6-7. Interview a news source

Interview a source who has been in the news or one who frequently deals with the media. The purpose of your interview is to ask the source about his or her experiences with the media. You are responsible for learning some background about your source. You will need to ask follow-up questions, and you should seek specific examples of good and bad experiences the source has had with the media. For example, if your source says some person or some newspaper or television station never treats him or her fairly, get examples of what the source means – questions asked, specific stories, and so on. After you conduct your interview, write a report

20

(make sure you include background about your source). To encourage candor from your source, you may tell the source this report is for a class assignment and not for publication.   Here are some questions to guide you:

1. How often do you come in contact with the media?

2. With whom are your contacts (local newspaper and radio, regional newspapers and TV, state media, national media)?

3. How long have you had press contact? Is it steady or intermittent?

4. Describe your other roles in the past in which you had press coverage.

5. What subjects have you been interviewed about most frequently.

6. Are most of your interviews in person or by telephone? Which do you prefer and why?

7. Do you ever contact the press? Why or why not? Give examples, if you do.

8. Overall, describe the fairness, accuracy and completeness of the reporters with whom you have dealt. How does the coverage differ for newspapers, radio, television or magazines?

9. Tell me about any bad experiences you have had with interviewers.   Describe examples of interviewing techniques and reporting that you considered bad interviewing techniques. (Here you will need to seek specifics from your source for the most complete explanation you can get.) What, if any, experiences have you had with poorly worded or unclear questions, misinterpretation of your position or inaccurate quotes? Discuss any personality conflict or bias you thought the interviewer had.

10. In situations in which you might not have been presented as positively as you would have liked, was the coverage fair and accurate? Explain.

11. What general complaints do you have about interviews?

12. Describe the good interviews you have had. How has the interviewer made the session effective?

13. What suggestions about interviewing do you have for reporters?

Leads and Nut Graphs

7

Copy and paste the following exercises in Word and write your leads in a Word document.

7-1. Hard-news (summary) leads

These leads summarize the main point of the story. Choose the most important elements of who, what, where, when, why or how, but don't clutter your lead with all these elements. Place points of emphasis (the most interesting or important information) at the beginning of the sentence. Read the following information, and write a one-sentence summary lead for each item.

1. A survey was released yesterday by the Child Abuse Prevention Center in Baltimore. The survey shows that three to four children die every day in the United States from child abuse or neglect. Statistics in the survey show that the number of child abuse or neglect cases reported at the end of this year rose to 2.7 million, from 2.5 million the previous year. More than half of the children who died were under age 1. Seventy-nine percent of the deaths were among children under age 5.

2. MILWAUKEE – For the past three days nearly 2,500 people have been demonstrating outside of an abortion clinic here. Some demonstrators support the clinic and others oppose it. Yesterday nearly 150 of the anti-abortion protesters were arrested. Police said they were arrested on disorderly conduct charges of blocking the entrances to the clinic. The protesters said they planned to demonstrate for six weeks. (Clue: Avoid starting with a numeral.)

3. This information comes from police. A delivery driver for a Chinese food restaurant was taking food to an apartment in your town yesterday. The apartment complex was at 718 S.W. Western Ave. The driver was robbed of the Chinese food at gunpoint. The driver works for The Great Wall of China Restaurant at 1336 S.W. 17th St. A man opened the outside security door to let the delivery driver in, and then the man disappeared. A short time later, the man came back and pointed a gun at the delivery driver. The man threatened to kill the driver unless he handed over the food. The driver gave it to him and ran out of the apartment building. Police weren't sure what specific food dishes the driver was carrying.

4. A fire in your town caused $45,000 in damages to a two-bedroom home in the 2300 block of Main Street. Fire officials said the fire was started by a lighted cigarette on a sofa. Firefighters arrived at the house at 3:30 a.m. and found it on fire. They had the blaze under control in five minutes. The homeowner, Kathy Mahoney, was awakened by the smoke and flames. She suffered minor burns on her hands and feet.

5. The state Bureau of Investigation [in your state] yesterday released a report of crime rates for the first three months of the year. The report says murders in your state are up 53 percent and violent crime increased 2 percent. The state bureau officials said the number of rapes and robberies decreased significantly.

6. A United Nations scientific panel released a report yesterday. Researchers of the United Nations Environment Program found that damage to the earth's ozone layer is increasing. They predicted that ozone levels could drop 3 percent in the next decade, which would lead to a 10-percent increase in skin cancer. The ozone layer above the earth absorbs some of the sun's cancer-causing ultraviolet rays.

7. Information comes from police in Santa Ana, Calif. A Santa Ana woman was charged with attempted murder yesterday. She was being held in the Orange County jail after being unable to post $250,000 bond. Police said the woman, June Carter, 71, doused her husband, who was confined to a wheelchair and had cancer, with rubbing alcohol and set him on fire. Police said she was angry because he ate her chocolate Easter bunny. She called paramedics six hours after the attack on her husband. Paul Carter, 62, was taken to the University of California Irvine Burn Center with third-degree burns, police said.

8. *Clue:* Choose one angle and don't flood your lead with statistics:
What: Broadband user surpassed the number of people using dial-up Internet access in the United States this year; 53 percent of residential users are now using broadband – source is Nielsen/NetRatings.
Why: Prices of broadband dropped. Elaboration: Surveys from the Pew Internet and American Life Project found that 69 percent of broadband users go online on a typical day, compared with 51 percent for dial-up. Broadband users who went online averaged 107 minutes surfing the Web, checking e-mail and otherwise engaged, 21 minutes longer than dial-up users. The United States trailed 12 of the 15 top countries, including Canada, in broadband penetration, according to a September report from U.N. International Telecommunication Union. South Korea topped the list at more than double the U.S. rate.

9. *Who:* Princeton University. ***What:*** Initiated a crackdown on high grades. ***When:*** This school year. ***Why:*** To stem grade inflation. ***How:*** The university put a cap on the number of A's that can be awarded. Previously, there was no official limit to the number of A's handed out, and nearly half the grades in an average Princeton class have been A-pluses, A's or A-minuses. Now, each department can give A's to no more than 35 percent of its students each semester.

10: Write a hard-news lead from this news release: According to the National Sleep Foundation, approximately 70 million people in the United States are affected by a sleep problem. Approximately 12 million Americans have restless legs syndrome, a sleep and movement disorder characterized by unpleasant (tingling, crawling, creeping and/or pulling) feelings in the legs, which cause an urge to move in order to relieve the symptoms. As many as 47 million adults may be putting themselves at risk for injury, health and behavior problems because they aren't meeting their minimum sleep need in order to be fully alert the next day. And, sleep deprivation and sleep disorders are estimated to cost Americans over $100 billion annually. Many experts agree on common sense sleeping tips such as avoiding caffeine, alcohol, and nicotine before bedtime, getting proper exercise, setting up a regular bedtime routine, and setting up a quiet, comfortable bedroom environment for proper sleeping conditions.

23

7-2. Delayed identification leads

When the person in your lead is not well known, you can delay identifying him or her until the second paragraph. Instead of using a name in the lead, you can identify the person by age, occupation (or affiliation with a group), location or some description. Write delayed identification leads as directed.

1. Use age as your delayed identification factor. Use your city as the location and yesterday as your time frame. Information comes from police. Police said John Cryer's tears may have saved him. Cryer was 13. He was walking in the 2700 block of S.E. 10th St. about 5:25 p.m. when a car containing four people pulled alongside. The driver displayed a blue semiautomatic handgun and demanded the boy's jacket. The boy was wearing a Chicago Bulls jacket. The boy started crying. The driver said, "Never mind," and the car left. No one was hurt or arrested.

Based on a story from *The Topeka Capital-Journal.* Used with permission.

2. Use occupation or organization affiliation as your delayed identification factor. Mike Haney spoke at your university yesterday. He is a founder of the American Indian Movement. He urged the audience to support a ban on using Indian names and symbols as mascots in sports. He said that using Indians as mascots promotes racism. "If all the kids see are those guys out there in the parking lot with makeup on their faces and dyed chicken feathers doing the war whoop, or they just see those TV westerns, that's how they'll perceive us," he said.

Based on a story from *The Topeka Capital-Journal.* Used with permission.

3. Use location as your delayed identification factor. John Sony, 69, was in critical condition at St. Francis Hospital and Medical Center yesterday. He is from Emporia (or use your town). He was diagnosed with Legionnaires' disease, which state health officials suspect he contracted at his high school reunion. Legionnaires' disease can cause a severe form of pneumonia. The disease was first identified in 1976 when 34 people died after attending an American Legion convention in a Philadelphia hotel.

Based on a story from *The Topeka Capital-Journal.* Used with permission.

4. Use a descriptive identifier for delayed identification. Information is from police reports. A man unsuccessfully tried to rob an eastside grocery store with a handgun last night. The man was wearing a white sack over his face. He entered the store and demanded money from the cashier at Food 4 Less at 3110 S.E. 6th. St. The cashier leaned against the alarm button. The suspect fled but was captured within an hour. He is Jack Fastrun of 2500 Easy St. He was charged with attempted robbery.

5. Use occupation or location for delayed identification. Audrey Feline, 50, a former animal control police officer (use your town), was arrested after authorities found 67 dead cats in her home. Police said the dead cats were in the woman's refrigerator and freezer. She was charged with 67 counts of misdemeanor animal abandonment.

7-3. Updated leads – forward spin

Updated leads give a forward spin to the news by stressing what is happening now or what will happen next instead of what happened yesterday. Writing this way is also called "advancing" the lead. This technique is almost always used in broadcast journalism and is often used online when news is constantly updated. Using the following information, write updated leads for print, broadcast or online delivery.

1. The faculty senate voted to require all undergraduates at your school to take courses in cultural diversity. The requirement goes into effect next fall and will begin with the freshman class.

2. (Use a delayed identification as well as an advance lead.) Police report that a man in your town was stabbed in a convenience store in your town last night. He is in fair condition at the hospital in your town today. Police said that Aristide Roberto, 43, was shopping in the Stop and Shop on 450 Elm St. at 2 a.m. last night when a man wearing a jogging suit stabbed him and fled. The assailant has not been found.

3. A 24-year-old man in your community was shot by a state trooper who returned fire in an early morning incident, state troopers said. The man, James Risky, was out on parole after being sentenced to five years in prison for pulling a loaded gun on three police officers. In today's incident, the trooper ordered Risky to get out of a stolen car and Risky fired a shot at him, troopers said. The trooper then fired back. Risky is in critical condition in the local (use your community) hospital.

4. A Santana High School freshman opened fire with a revolver, killing two students and wounding another 13 people Monday. The 15-year-old boy later surrendered to police officers without incident. He will be arraigned as an adult in San Diego Superior Court on Wednesday. He is being charged with first-degree murder.

5. An American Airlines flight was delayed more than three hours before takeoff Sunday after a fake grenade used to test security screening fell out of a carry-on bag and rolled down the aisle, an airport spokeswoman said. A woman was in custody and authorities were trying to determine how she ended up with a bag belonging to a security screener that contained the phony grenade, said Rita Vandergaw, spokeswoman for the Unified Port of San Diego.

7-4. Impact leads

An impact lead tells readers how the story will affect them. Sometimes you may use the word "you" in your lead to personalize the impact, but you also can use a noun, such as "residents" or "voters" or whoever will be affected by the action in the story. Write impact leads for the following information for print or broadcast delivery.

1. The U.S. Army Corps of Engineers is conducting a program to install free plastic covering for roofs of homes damaged during the recent hurricane. There are five more days to apply for the program. Homeowners whose roofs were damaged during the storm may sign up for the free roof repair at any of the corps offices.

2. The City Council (use your community's local governing body) is considering an ordinance to outlaw parking of vehicles in front yards and unpaved side yards. The ordinance would allow vehicles to be parked on private property only if they are on asphalt or concrete driveways. If residents have a gravel driveway, they would be forced to park in the street if the ordinance is adopted. Councilwoman Carol Schuman, like more than 50 percent of the homeowners in her district, has a gravel driveway. She is opposed to the ordinance. "Where am I supposed to park my car?" she said. The council took the ordinance under consideration and will discuss it again at its next meeting.

Based on a story from *The Topeka Capital-Journal*. Used with permission.

3. The Missouri Board of Curators approved a new tuition rate for the University of Missouri. The tuition will increase 12 percent. That's equivalent to $240 more a year. The increase affects students at all four campuses of the university: Columbia, St. Louis, Rolla and Kansas City. The increase was necessary to help cover a $14 million increase in expenses, said University President C. Peter McGrath. Under the new rate schedule, full-time students who are Missouri residents will pay $67.20 a credit hour. They now pay $60 a credit hour. Juniors and seniors will pay $74.30 a credit hour. They now pay $66.30.

Based on a story from the *St. Louis Post-Dispatch*. Used with permission.

4. The oldest subway system in the nation has moved into the 21st century with a plan to replace metal tokens with computerized fare cards, officials said. The Massachusetts Bay Transportation Authority installed an automated fare collection system at a cost of $120 million. The new system will offer riders ``smart cards'' that passengers wave in front of scanners. Riders will keep their cards and reload them through automated machines, the Internet or the telephone.

5. Researchers have developed a drug that speeds recovery from the common cold. The drug, to be sold by prescription under the brand name Picovir, eases cold symptoms within a day and makes a runny nose completely clear up a day sooner than usual.

7-5. Broadcast leads

If you are in a course that stresses convergence of print and broadcast writing, write the previous leads for broadcast delivery, as your instructor wishes. To convert them to broadcast, use active voice and update them to emphasize what is happening now.

7-6. Attribution in leads

Decide whether attribution is or is not needed in the following leads by writing yes or no:

_____ **1.** An employment workshop for foreign students will be at 3:30 p.m. today in the student union.

_____ **2.** Students will receive their enrollment permits in the mail this fall instead of waiting in line for them.

_____ **3.** A fire that caused an estimated $150,000 damage to a home in the western part of the city was caused by a lighted cigarette on a sofa.

_____ **4.** A man shot and killed his wife because he was convinced she was having an affair with his best friend.

_____ **5.** A woman was arrested and charged with hitting a police officer in the face with her key ring.

_____ **6.** A 28-year-old man bashed a relative's car with a baseball bat Saturday night in a dispute over a baseball card.

7-7. Soft leads

Soft leads usually can be classified as descriptive, anecdotal or narrative. Many times a soft lead will have a combination of these qualities. Using some of the leads in your textbook as models, write soft leads as indicated.

1. Write a soft lead, using any technique you wish.

A man in your town was charged yesterday with battery to a law enforcement officer and obstructing official duty. The man was named Harley Dudley Surritte. He was 42 years old and lived at 2313 S.W. Mission Road. He was released on $1,000 bond last night from the county jail. Police said he threw a 2-by-3-foot velvet painting of Elvis Presley off the wall and threw it at officer Chuck Haggard's head. Police said they were sent to Surritte's home at 3:49 p.m. on a report of a domestic fight. Police said Surritte told them he didn't like police officers. "It's the only known Elvis sighting by law enforcement officers in this area," a (your town) police officer said yesterday.
Based on a story from *The Topeka Capital-Journal*. Used with permission.

2. Using the focus-on-a-person technique, write an anecdotal lead for this information and include your nut graph.

PHASE is an acronym for Project for Homemakers in Arizona Seeking Employment. It is a program that offers women who have near-poverty level incomes vocational training in largely male-dominated fields such as construction. More than 4,000 single parents and displaced homemakers have received vocational training from the program in the past two years. Jane Johnson used to be a long-distance operator. She answered telephones eight hours a day. She received vocational training through the program. Now she straps on a tool belt and a hard hat and heads for work at local construction sites as a carpentry apprentice. She is 35.

3. Write a descriptive "show-in-action" lead including the nut graph.

Your community has a home renovation program called Model Block. It is for homeowners who are elderly or disadvantaged and unable to repair their homes. This past weekend 45 people in three neighborhoods in your community were treated to free exterior home remodeling as part of that program. Robert Thompson was one of them. He stood on his newly repaired porch and watched as volunteers, with tools and paintbrushes, scurried around his neighborhood. Thompson and his wife, Flora, were unable to pay for repairs to their home after a van hit the side of their house more than a year ago. Matters became worse when Flora Thompson suffered a stroke that left her paralyzed on her left side. About 400 volunteers took part in the program to give free repairs during the weekend.

Based on a story in *The Topeka Capital-Journal*. Used with permission.

4. Write a narrative lead (reconstructing the event) for the following information:

You are writing an anniversary story about Pearl Harbor, Dec. 7, 1941. On that day, Japanese fighter pilots bombed Pearl Harbor in Hawaii, killing 2,471 Americans and drawing the United States into World War II. The Japanese lost 55 men. You interview a World War II veteran, Earl Schaeffer. On that date he was 19 years old and he was Pvt. Earl Schaeffer. He was stationed at Hickam Field in Oahu, Hawaii.

He tells you what he was doing on Dec. 7, 1941. He says it was a quiet Sunday morning. He was sitting at the switchboard at Hickam Field in Oahu, Hawaii. He says not a single phone call came across the wire. The only sound was the voice on the radio, speaking during the "Lutheran Hour." He says he was studying a book about aerial navigation. He wanted to be a fighter pilot. He began to hear sounds of bombing. It hardly drew his attention. Practice maneuvers were common around the base. But the noise grew louder and louder.

"I ran out of the hangar and I saw aircraft swooping down and dropping black objects, and it still didn't dawn on me, because I wasn't expecting anything like that." Then he saw the large red circles painted on the side of the planes, the symbol of Japanese fighter planes. Based on a story from *The Salina* (Kan.) *Journal*. Used with permission.

28

5. Write a mystery teaser lead for this information.

The County Commission in your community voted 2-1 yesterday to pass an ordinance banning ownership of 16 species of animals "not normally domesticated," including tigers, lions, bears, elephants, wolves,   primates, alligators and crocodiles. The commission's action was prompted by complaints from neighbors of Delores Sampson.   To Sampson, her pet named Marriaha is "like any other kitten." She says Marriaha is always trying to jump up on her lap. But there is one big difference between Marriaha and other 22-month-old cats. Marriaha is a 300-pound Bengal tiger. In December Marriaha escaped from a cage on the back porch and traipsed around her front lawn, separated from her neighbor's yard by just a 4-foot high chain-link fence.

Based on a story from *The* (Louisville, Ky.) *Courier-Journal.* Used with permission.

6. Convert these summary leads to soft leads:

a. A student at a private school in Vermont disrobed in the middle of her graduation speech. Her name was Kate Logan. She was 18. The school was Long Trail School in Dorset, Vermont. She said she made the decision several months before graduation when she was searching for some way to mark the significance of the event. She stepped to the front of the graduation podium and talked of her journey to a road less traveled. Then she slipped out of her graduation robe and finished her speech naked. School officials were not amused.

b. A growing practice in publishing is making it harder for students to resell their textbooks. The practice is called "bundling," a method of packaging a textbook with supplemental materials such as CD-ROMs. When a book is bundled with a supplement, its ISBN number changes in a database. ISBN stands for International Standard Book Number. Bookstores will only buy back books with ISBNs that match the numbers in a database. Tara Reynold, a senior at a university in the Midwest, is unhappy about that. She says the supplements aren't necessary. "The teachers don't encourage or enforce their use," she says.

Adapted from a story in *The University Daily Kansan.*

c. The facts: A Jamaican hotel is trying to appeal to couples who want to get married. The hotel is offering a nude wedding package for Valentines' Day this year. For $470 a night, the SuperClubs' Hedonism II Resort in Runaway Bay, Jamaica, will provide the minister, the marriage license, the cake and music without charge. You won't need to buy a tuxedo or wedding dress. And you won't need any sunblock.

d. A new study shows that humans can spread germs to their pets. The study shows that cats and dogs can catch bad things from their owners. Canadian researchers documented 16 cases of dangerous, hard-to-treat staph infections in horses, cats and dogs. They believe that all of them probably began with owners or veterinarians infecting the animals.

e. Chocolate is unhealthy for dogs. Dr. Melanie Landis, a veterinarian at the College of Veterinary Medicine and Biomedical Sciences, Texas A&M University, says chocolate could cause your dog stomach aches or irregularities in heart function. "Dark and baking chocolates have the highest concentrations and should be strictly avoided," Landis warns. "Even in small amounts, these chocolates can be toxic.

Story Organization 8

8-1. Pacing and parallelism

Copy and paste these paragraphs into a new Word document or print them and rewrite them in your word processor. These excerpts are from a story by Ken Fuson, the *Des Moines Register* writer featured in this chapter of your textbook. The paragraphs have been rewritten for this exercise to make the sentences cumbersome. Rewrite these paragraphs to improve the pacing as Fuson might have written them, mixing long and short sentences and using parallelism. You may split the paragraphs here into several paragraphs if you think that will improve the pacing. Read your rewritten material aloud to make sure it has good rhythm.

a. PANORA, Ia. – This small town welcomed home one of its soldiers Friday, but instead of jubilant well-wishers, there were 525 mourners who packed every corner of the United Methodist Church, and instead of a parade down Main Street, there was a stream of cars that stretched from the church to the West Cemetery outside of town.

b. There were flags at half-staff, there were red, white and blue ribbons tied to flower sprays that surrounded the altar and there were tears – of grief, not joy.

c. To the rest of the country, Army Spec. Michael Mills was one of 191 Americans killed in the war, he was one of 28 people killed Feb. 25 when an Iraqi suicide bomb exploded, but to the 1,100 people here, Mike Mills was the 23-year-old hometown boy who carried on a family tradition by joining the Army, and his funeral Friday provided a somber contrast to the joyous reunions held for returning troops throughout the country.

Adapted from a story by Ken Fuson, "Amid euphoria, town mourns soldier's return." The *Des Moines* (Iowa) *Register and Tribune Co.* Used with permission.

8-2. Endings

a. Write a circle kicker (a quote or statement that relates to the lead). The first two paragraphs are the original lead. The remaining information is out of order.

In seventh grade, Christine Arguello read a magazine article about lawyers. The article specifically mentioned Harvard Law School. She decided at that moment she wanted to be a lawyer and she wanted to attend Harvard.

In fact, Harvard was the only law school she applied to after receiving her undergraduate degree in elementary education in 1980 from the University of Colorado.

She practiced law for 11 years in Colorado Springs. Arguello received the 1991 Hispanic of the Year Award in Colorado and was involved in the Colorado Springs community. She often wonders where she would be if she had not read the magazine article about law school.

Being Hispanic was an advantage, Arguello said.

"At times, I had to be twice as good as the next person," she said. "I used it positively and did not dwell on it."

Arguello, who specialized in bankruptcy and commercial litigation, was the first minority to become a partner in the prestigious Denver-based law firm, Holland and Hart. She was also the first Hispanic to be hired by any of the four biggest law firms in Denver.

Based on a story from *The University Daily Kansan.* Used with permission.

b. Write a future kicker; select a paragraph from the story or write your own ending.

Topeka resident Gary Henson may have the largest Batman collection in the world. He hasn't met anybody with more Batman merchandise. His collection contains about 4,000 items. Henson believes Batman's mortality is one reason for his popularity.

Henson, who has owned Quality Carpet Cleaning since 1975, would like to eventually open a Batman museum. He would charge $1 admission only for one reason – so he could buy more Batman merchandise. Henson, 47, has a wide variety of Batman memorabilia, including rare items from the 1960s, such as Batman and Robin bubble bath containers and a Batman lamp.

Based on a story from *The Topeka Capital-Journal.* Used with permission.

c. Write a quote kicker for this story:

A man in your community died last month. After his death, your local county Department of Social Services sent him a letter. The man's name was Albert Maxwell. The man's brother, Jason Maxwell, said the letter is "living proof of how screwed up the system is." The letter said: "Your food stamps will be stopped effective in January because we received a notice that you passed away. You may reapply if there is a change in your circumstances. May God bless you." Rose Josephson, director of the county's social service system, said it's not the fault of her agency. She said the form letter was generated by a computer. She said a caseworker added the "May God bless you," because the employee wanted to soften the message.

d. Write a factual kicker for this story; attribute the information to a police report in your town.

Police arrested a 24-year-old man from your town on charges of burglary. The suspect broke into a Domino's pizza parlor on 1700 W. 23rd St. Sunday night. He told police that he had not had anything to eat since Friday night. He said, "I was hungry." It was not known whether the suspect got anything to eat. The man had raided the restaurant cooler. The cooler contained three plastic containers of pizza sauce, 10 pounds of mozzarella cheese and two sacks of flour. A store manager who lives across the street had called the police.

8-3. Revision to tighten and correct style

This story has many extraneous words and style errors. Before you submit your stories to your editor or professor, you should revise them by checking for accuracy and tightening your writing, as in this exercise. Edit or rewrite this story by eliminating wordiness and correcting style errors.

A woman named Shirley Anne Hall has up until December 8 to clear up her Garden Grove house of rotten oranges that have gone bad, cobwebs, vehicle parts, musty newspapers and a year's worth of dirty dishes that have not been washed.

Hall, who is age 54, must remove overgrown weeds in her yard and other debris from her yard, which is located in the 12,000 block of Barlett Street, Orange County, superior court judge Randell Wilkinson said on Wednsday. If she fails to comply with the order which judge Randell Wilkinson made on Wednesday, the city will bring in work crews and send Hall the bill for the work the crews have done.

The city has been trying to persuade Hall to sort through her mess since the year of 1988, city attorney Stuart Scudder said.

Hall, a woman who is diagnosed with chronic depression, said the city is harrassing her and that the stress that the city has caused her by harrassing her has prevented her from making any progress.

The Dayle McIntosh Center for the Disabled in Anaheim is looking for volunteers who of their own volition will offer to help Hall to clean up.

Adapted from a story in *The Orange County* (Calif.) *Register.* Used with permission.

Story Forms

9

Copy and paste these exercises into a new Word document or print them out so you have the information; then write stories in the formats as directed.

9-1. Inverted pyramid exercise

Write this story in inverted pyramid order, placing the most newsworthy information first and the rest in descending order of importance. Use a summary lead. You may substitute your town for Portland. Put your quotes in separate paragraphs, unless you have two quotes from the same speaker.

Information from the Portland Fire Bureau: A canister of tear gas was set off by vandals (yesterday morning) at the Gregory Heights Middle School. Three students are being sought for questioning. At least 48 children and two teachers were taken to a dozen Portland hospitals for treatment. The fire department was called at 9:31 a.m. A second alarm was sounded at 10:32 a.m. The problem caused no evacuation of homes in the neighborhood around the school. The school is located at Northeast 73rd Avenue and Siskiyou Street.

Students and teachers vomited and suffered a number of other problems, including a burning sensation in the lungs, nose, throat and eyes, due to the gas that apparently was released in a school corridor. The school was closed for the day. The Fire Bureau began allowing staff members to return inside about noon.

From Don Mayer, spokesman for the Portland Fire Bureau: He said the trips to the hospital were precautionary. He didn't know if anyone was in serious or critical condition. "The symptoms the kids are exhibiting are consistent with Mace." He said a Mace-like container was given to investigators by a parent who said it was sold to her son on the school grounds yesterday morning. Mace is a type of tear gas. He said school officials gave investigators the names of three possible suspects. He said investigators were trying to reach those youths.

From the school Principal John Alkire: He said the substance was in the science and math hall area in the northwest corner of the school's first floor. He said the substance was odorless. "It was like walking into an irritating wall."

From Nguyen Do, an eighth grader: He was in class during the morning break. He said he and others went out in the hall and started coughing. "So I covered my mouth and ran out of the building. It's Mace. I know that. It was a set-up to get out of class or something."

From Michael Grice, spokesman for the Portland Public Schools: Students who were not affected by the fumes were sent home about 10:45 a.m. The school district sent buses to take the students home. Classes at the school will resume tomorrow [use the day of the week].

From Jessie Doty, 12, a seventh-grader: "I started coughing. It just stung my throat. My eyes watered and turned red."

From Jeff MacMillan, 12, a seventh-grader: He said he got a headache from the chemical. He said other classmates were worse off, including one girl who fainted and had to be carried from the building.

From Autumn Gierlich, 13, an eighth-grader who suffers from asthma: She was coughing and receiving oxygen shortly after the incident when you arrived at the school. You notice her waiting for an ambulance and you get these comments from her: "I got the stuff into my lungs, and I could barely breathe. I had to gasp for air. I was dizzy. Now I'm feeling better. They gave me oxygen. I coughed and coughed, and spit up phlegm."

From Richard Harder, a paramedic with the Portland Fire Bureau: He said he was one of the first to arrive. He said he saw about 15 children on the ground. Some of them had severe respiratory problems. Others were coughing, vomiting and sneezing.

From Carol Palumbo, an eighth-grade teacher: She was consoling crying students in front of the school after the evacuation. "The kids are really upset. It's just horrendous, whatever it was."

From your observations and basic questions: Students were taken to an area on the front lawn of the school. They were carried by stretcher or walked to ambulances. The children were ages 12 to 15. More than a dozen ambulances were sent to the school. The school is located at Northeast 73rd Avenue and Siskiyou Street. It has more than 900 staff members and students in the 6th, 7th and 8th grades.

Based on a story by Dave Hogan and Paul Koberstein, *The Oregonian.* Used with permission.

9-2. *Wall Street Journal* formula

For this exercise, use an anecdotal lead, nut graph and supporting points for this story as discussed in your textbook. You do not have to change the wording in this story; just reorganize the paragraphs in *The Wall Street Journal* formula order. Plan your order topically, and use the kiss-off technique, blocking information from each source. If the information is not enclosed in quotation marks, the comments are not direct quotes.

General notes:

Nutritionists agree it's understandable that students that who stay up late to study need to eat to keep going. In their newsletters, nutritionists suggest that fruit or even pretzels would be healthier snacks than candy or pizza. The fabled Freshman 15 affects men and women, according to students. Those nasty 10 to 15 pounds that students tend to gain in the first few months of college have become as much a part of higher education as reading lists and blue-book exams.

Many schools send new students another helpful message during orientation: Find time between study and socializing to exercise every day, be it through sports, aerobics classes or a simple walk. Some schools, such as the University of Pennsylvania and Rutgers University, offer special workshops to freshmen to help them avoid the weight gain.

Gene Lamm, a junior at Beaver College in Glenside: "I've gained 20 pounds since I left home." He made the comment as he shared an entire chocolate cake with two friends. "I used to have abs (abdominal muscles); I don't know what happened to them," Lamm said, chuckling, as he lifted his gray T-shirt.

Peg Abell, a nutritionist at Widener University: Often students eat out of stress and even more often in an effort to socialize and fit in. "Some people eat to feel better since eating can have a soothing effect, and some use eating as a way of maintaining control of at least one portion of their life."

Joe Leung, a junior at Villanova: "I went up for second portions every day. I weighed 115 when I came, and I got up to 140."

Missy Palko, a sophomore at Beaver College: "I gained 30 pounds last year. If you look in the closets around here, they're all packed with food." An informal survey of dorm residents proved her right. Room after room held stashes of cheese crackers, doughnuts, popcorn, frosted breakfast cereals, chocolate and sodas.

Vanessa Varvarezis, a freshman who had been at Villanova only three weeks at the time of this interview: "I think I've already gained it. My parents sent me away with four bags of junk food, and it's almost half gone already." Eating at Donahue Hall one recent evening, Varvarezis had spaghetti, garlic bread, vegetables, about eight cookies and a fudge ice cream pop. "It was Weight Watchers, though," she said about the dessert. According to a calorie chart given out by the Villanova food services staff, Varvarezis had eaten more than 900 calories for dinner. And that was before the late-night pizza run. "I order out a lot," Varvarezis said.

Jim Martin, manager of California Style Pizza, near Villanova University: "We call them the pie hours." From 9 p.m. to 2 a.m., he said, his six employees deliver up to 50 pizzas per hour to the nearby campus. He routinely makes four extra pizzas for them to take along and sell on the spot. He said his delivery people have no trouble "hawking pizzas."

Stephen Bailey, a sociology professor who conducted a weight-gain study for Tufts University in Massachusetts with Tufts nutrition professor Jeanne Goldberg: They tracked 120 women through their first year of college. He said the Freshman 15 is a myth. "Basically we came up with some results that surprised us. On average, the women gained a little bit less than a pound. They gained a bit between the fall and spring and lost all of that over the course of the summer." The participants were volunteers.

Adapted from a story in *The Philadelphia Inquirer.* Used with permission

9-3. Hourglass exercise

Write this story in hourglass form, starting with a hard-news lead. Then proceed in chronological order for a portion or the rest of the story. You do not have to use all the information. The point of this exercise is to decide when and where you will begin the chronology.

You are making routine calls to the fire department and you receive this report from the dispatcher. Attribute information to fire department officials. Write the story in inverted pyramid order or hourglass form. Use yesterday as your time frame.

Information comes from Neil Heesacker, a spokesman for the fire department in your community. Firefighters responded to a fire at an apartment in a 32-unit apartment complex, Anderson Villa apartments, at 15758 S.E. Division St. at 6:39 a.m. The fire was brought under control at 7:05 a.m. The blaze caused an estimated $50,000 to the apartment building and $10,000 damage to the contents of the apartment. The value of the apartment building is estimated at $480,000. The family's belongings in the apartment that burned were valued at $80,000.

The apartment was rented by Linda Lee Fuson. Her two sons, Kenneth A. J. Fuson, 10, and Michael Fuson, 14, were in the apartment at the time of the fire. Linda Fuson was not. She arrived some time after 6:40 a.m. Her whereabouts before then are unknown. The fire burned through the floor and blistered the gypsum walls and melted the family's television set. Three pet birds died.

The fire also caused smoke damage to the apartment of Pat and Lisa Hampton, who live across the stairs from the Fuson family. The cause of the fire is under investigation. A neighbor, Darren Nitz, 31, is credited with saving Michael Fuson's life. He lives on the first floor, just below the Fusons' apartment. Michael Fuson suffered burns over a third of his body. He is in critical condition at Emanuel Hospital and Health Center's burn unit. He has second- and third-degree burns on his hands, arms, face, neck, back, buttocks and thighs. Kenneth Fuson was trapped in his bedroom. He died in the fire. Fire in an enclosed area such as an apartment can push temperatures to 1,700 degrees Fahrenheit near the ceiling and 1,000 degrees on the floor.

Information from interview with Darren Nitz: "About 6:35 a.m. I heard neighbors pounding on my door and yelling about the fire. I didn't think much about it at first, until someone said two children were trapped in the apartment. Michael was about seven feet from his bedroom door. He was saying 'I can't, I can't,' and rolling over and over. I said, 'We've got to get out of here.' I tried to grab hold of his arm but couldn't because he was so badly burned. I put him over my shoulder and carried him outside. He told me that Kenneth was still upstairs. I went back to the top of the stairs but the flames reached the front door. Another neighbor, Brad Lindsey, grabbed a fire extinguisher and followed me."

From Brad Lindsey, 24: "It was fully going when we got up there. Just after we got up them, it just vacuumed and shot right across the stairway. Nitz and I went back down the stairs. There was no way either of us could do anything about it."

Based on a story from *The Oregonian.* Used with permission.

9-4. List technique

Lists are often used to clarify bureaucratic stories, especially those containing numbers. Write this story using the list technique. Your story will be accompanied by a chart. You may use several lists in this story.

The U.S. Census Bureau has released a report about the value of a college education. The report is based on data on educational trends and attainment levels are shown by characteristics such as age, sex, race, Hispanic origin, marital status, occupation, industry, nativity and, if foreign-born, when they entered the country. The tables also describe the relationship between earnings and educational attainment.

Although the statistics are primarily at the national level, some data are shown for regions and states. The data demonstrate the extent to which having such a degree pays off: average earnings in 2008 totaled $83,144 for those with an advanced degree, compared with $58,613 for those with a bachelor's degree only. People whose highest level of attainment was a high school diploma had average earnings of $31,283.

Overall, 87 percent of adults 25 and older had a high school diploma or more in 2009, with 30 percent holding at least a bachelor's degree. Among women 25 and older with a bachelor's degree or more, 65 percent were married with a spouse present. The corresponding rate for men was 71 percent. For women and men with advanced degrees, the corresponding percentages were 66 percent and 76 percent.

The number of U.S. residents with bachelor's degrees or more climbed 34 percent between 1999 and 2009, from 43.8 million to 58.6 million. More than half (53 percent) of Asians 25 and older had a bachelor's degree or more, much higher than the rate for non-Hispanic whites (33 percent), blacks (19 percent) and Hispanics (13 percent).

Among young adults 25 to 29, 35 percent of women and 27 percent of men possessed a bachelor's degree or more in 2009. This gap has grown considerably in the last decade: it was only 3 percentage points in 1999 (30 percent for women, 27 percent for men).

Also included are data on the highest level of education achieved by a wide range of demographic and socioeconomic characteristics, including age, sex, race, Hispanic origin, marital status, household relationship, citizenship, nativity and year of entry. Historical tables provide data on mean earnings by attainment level, sex, race and Hispanic origin with data back to 1975, and tables on attainment levels back to 1940.

This report confirms an earlier report released in 2002 from the Commerce Department's Census Bureau's Economic and Statistics Administration that says a college master's degree is worth $1.3 million more in a lifetime than a high school diploma.

Based on a news release from the U.S. Census Bureau.

Storytelling and Feature Techniques

10

10-1. Feature Pulitzer Prize analysis

What would happen if one of the world's greatest violinists performed incognito in a Washington, D.C. metro station during rush hour? Would people stop and listen? Would anyone recognize him? That's what *The Washington Post* decided to explore, and the result was the 2008 Pulitzer Prize for feature writing. Analyze this story for feature writing techniques. Discuss the feature writing techniques such as the use of detail, description and what you think about a story that is contrived by newspaper. Write an analysis of this story, which you can access at *http://www.pulitzer.org* under 2008 feature writing category; click on Works and read "Pearls before breakfast."

10-2. Storytelling style for a crime story

Write this story using narrative writing style. Here are your notes:

It is the Christmas season. A woman was shopping at the Galleria shopping mall in Fort Lauderdale. A man robbed the woman after she got into her unlocked car. The suspect has not been caught. Police described him as a white man about 27 years old, 5 feet 7 inches tall, with brown hair and brown eyes. He was described as clean shaven but unkempt. He stole her wallet.

You interview the woman who was robbed. Her name is Pauline Cayia and she lives in Fort Lauderdale. She said she finished shopping about 7 p.m. Sunday and returned to her unlocked car at the Galleria mall. She said she had been shopping for about an hour and a half. She manages a recording studio. She said the robber was polite and well spoken. She said he took her wallet, but on Monday (a few hours before you interview her) she received a phone call that her wallet had been found. It was returned along with her credit cards and driver's license. Only her $85 in cash was missing.

She said as she got into her car, she smelled a strong body odor. She drove away from the shopping center at 2700 E. Sunrise Blvd. and a man popped up in the back seat and demanded her purse. She said the robber went through her purse as she was driving south along Federal Highway toward Broward Boulevard.

"Before I got in the car, I looked around and didn't see anything. I smelled an odor when I put my packages in the front seat, and I checked the back seat, but I didn't see anybody. I suppose he was sleeping, because he didn't say anything until I got to Federal Highway. He said, 'Ma'am, give

39

me your purse and let me off here.' I started going fast to try to attract the attention of a policeman, but I didn't find anybody to stop me. I was going fast, and he said, 'You're going to kill us.' "

When she was driving toward Broward Boulevard, the robber returned her purse. "He said, 'Here's your purse' and threw it into the front seat, but he kept my wallet."

At Federal and Broward, Cayia slowed to turn and ended up hitting a car. At that point, the robber jumped out and ran, even though the car was still moving. She drove directly to the police station. "I don't know if I was scared or in control. I just wanted to get the police."

Based on a story from the *Florida Sun-Sentinel* (Fort Lauderdale, Fla.). Used with permission.

10-3. Storytelling mindset exercises

a. Fiction to fact: Take any fiction short story that you like and write it in newspaper style using storytelling techniques. Short stories by Edgar Allan Poe could work well in this exercise. Check the Poe museum at *http://www.poemuseum.org*.

b. Fact like fiction: Using storytelling techniques but sticking to the facts, turn a story from the *National Enquirer* or any other supermarket tabloid into a newspaper story. You can find the *Enquirer* at *http://www.nationalenquirer.com*.

c. Fun facts: Take a basic news story from your campus or local newspaper and write it in the style of a supermarket tabloid newspaper.

10-4. Storytelling news feature

This storytelling exercise was devised by Alan Richman, former writer and writing coach for *The Boston Globe* and currently for *GQ (Gentlemen's Quarterly)* magazine. Richman wrote this story when he was at *The Globe*. His assignment was to follow up on a news story with a feature. The news story is reprinted here; then you will get Richman's notes. Use those notes to write a feature of no more than 750 words – about 16 inches in a newspaper story. The point of the exercise is to see how many details and rich quotes you can fit in that amount of space. As you read Richman's notes, consider how much detail he gathered. You will also have to decide if you should use anonymous sources.

The news story:

An East Boston man confessed to stealing a car last Thursday and spending most of the $10,000 in cash he found in the glove compartment before he was caught on Saturday, police said.

Michael Yanelli, 22, of 569 Bennington St., East Boston, was arrested at 9:15 Saturday night and charged with stealing a 1979 Cadillac belonging to Rene Gignac of Laconia, N.H.

The car, which had been discovered missing at 11:45 a.m. Thursday, had been parked in front of 880 Saratoga St., East Boston. Police said that besides a briefcase, papers and wallet on the seat of the car, the glove compartment contained $30,000 in checks and $10,000 in cash.

40

Yanelli's arrest came after a police investigation and tips from neighborhood contacts. A police spokesman said Yanelli admitted to the theft in a deposition and said he had spent most of the money he found. He turned over $2,682 in cash and $1,972 worth of plane tickets, the spokesman said.

Yanelli was charged with larceny over $100, and will be arraigned in East Boston District Court tomorrow morning, police said.

The Boston Globe. Used with permission.

.   .   .

Three days after this story appears an editor decides that it should be followed up. The editor wants to know: Who is this guy? How did he manage to spend more than $7,000 in less than two days? How does he feel about his windfall?

You are assigned to write the follow-up story.   All you know, in addition to what you read in the brief news story, is that Boston has one of the highest car theft rates in the United States, and East Boston, one of the neighborhoods within the city, has the highest car theft rate in Boston. It's a lower-middle class, blue-collar neighborhood.

You go out to report your story. This is what you find out:

.   .   .

Yanelli lives on a tree-lined residential street not far from Wonderland, a greyhound racetrack. A church, St. Mary's Star of the Sea, is across the street from his home. In the same building, below his apartment, is Carlo's Cold Cut Centre, a tiny neighborhood grocery. The building he lives in is a little seedy, with a broken window, ugly asphalt shingle sidings, no names on the mailboxes.

You talk to a teenage girl with deep lavender eye shadow. She is walking down the street. She won't give her name. She knows Yanelli, says he's a little slow. She says, "If I found $10,000, I wouldn't tell anyone. I'd get right out of the car."

You go to 880 Saratoga St., which is four blocks from his apartment. Its one address in a series of garden apartments called "Brandywine Village. You stop three elderly ladies walking down the street. They won't give their names, but they tell you that Gignac was helping his mother-in-law move and the money in the glove compartment was for a down payment on a new house or condominium for her.

"The daughter told me that," the first lady says.

"I wouldn't leave that money in a car," says the second. "I'd put it in my bloomers."

You go to the local police precinct, District Seven. They know Yanelli by reputation.

"He's a little addle-brained," one cop tells you.

The crime report is down at District 1, police headquarters. You call and find out that Yanelli is charged with larceny of a motor vehicle worth more than $9,000, stealing $10,060 in U.S. currency, stealing three credit cards and three checks. He pleaded not guilty and was sent to Charles Street Jail, the city jail. He did not post bail. His court attorney is Paul Luciano. You call him but he is out of town.

The detective investigating the case tells you, on background, that Yanelli destroyed the checks, kept the cash and bought two first-class airline tickets to Las Vegas for $1,800. He kept the money in a brown paper bag. He changed plates on the car. The tips came when he was seen flashing a lot of money around the neighborhood.

At the East District Court, people tell you that Yanelli is a big kid with a shaved head, a little slow.

You find it interesting that everyone you speak to tells you how dumb Yanelli was to keep the car. Everybody – even the policemen – says that he should have ditched the car as soon as he found the cash.

41

You try to call Rene Gignac in New Hampshire. He has an unlisted number.

The Charles Street Jail is run by the Suffolk County sheriff. You call and ask to speak to Yanelli. A public relations official for the sheriff's department says she will make the request. She says she will also advise Yanelli to talk to his lawyer before talking to you. You get lucky. Yanelli tries for more than a day, but his lawyer is still out of town. He says he'll talk to you. The following are your quotes from the interview:

You: What did you feel when you saw the money?

Yanelli: My heart went 90 miles an hour. — backup quote?

You: Describe what the money looked like.

Yanelli: It was about this big. (He makes a 4-inch space with his hands.) It was 100s, 50s, 10s. The glove compartment was open. There was a briefcase in the front seat with $60 in it.

You: Why did you steal the car in the first place?

Yanelli: A joyride. Just to take the car. It's a habit with me. It ain't going to happen anymore.

You: What did you think after you got in the car and were riding around?

Yanelli: This guy (Gignac) is so stupid. I got to talk to the guy. I've only been charged with larceny of a motor vehicle. I wasn't charged with stealing money. If I have to do any time, I want them to prove it. I have three previous larcenies of motor vehicles – all the cars had keys in them. One in Malden, one in East Boston, one in Winthrop. This is the fourth.

Yanelli continued: I drove away and noticed the car was on empty, so I went for gas. I opened the briefcase. There was $60 in it. I put $20 in and got half a tank. I opened the glove compartment, looking for something to blow my nose. I threw out a white envelope. 20s and 50s and 100s piled out.

You: What did you spend it on?

Yanelli: I was going to Vegas the next day. Thursday afternoon I had the money. I bought a couple of things, a color television for my best friend because he was getting married. I went out and bought $600 worth of clothes, paid back a couple of debts. The two airline tickets to Vegas cost $1,972. I was going to go, but didn't. I was going to take a friend but he said he wanted to stay home for the 4th of July. My brother said to me, "Get rid of the car." Yeah, I know, I know. Why didn't I? I almost did. I even drove to Revere (a small city adjoining Boston) on Thursday to Cerretani's parking lot (a grocery store), wiped my fingerprints off the car. I was throwing the keys away. I hesitated. I said no. I needed a couple more things. I went to lunch. I took a cab home. I went to the dog track, lost a couple hundred. Thursday night I went to Jeveli's (a restaurant) in East Boston and ate. I went home. Friday morning a friend of mine picked up the briefcase. He gets rid of the briefcase. This guy (Gignac) is completely stupid – there's $60,000 - $70,000 in money orders in the briefcase. The checkbook shows 80,000 bucks. I'm down on this guy. It's his fault. Friday morning I went back to get the car. A friend and I went to Suffolk Downs (a thoroughbred racing track in East Boston). I end up winning $1,500. I had the perfecta in the last race.

(The perfecta is a type of bet based on winning first and second place finishers. Note: You check the race results. In the 10th at Suffolk Downs, Fleet Concessioner, an 8-1 shot, finished first and Marshua's Romeo finished second. The perfecta paid $115 for a $2 bet.)

42

Yanelli: I said to my friend, "I'll go get my mother and father a color TV. A Sears TV." My mother turned it back. She wouldn't take it. I spent $1,700 on a TV for a friend's mother and father, a Sony Trinitron. I gave the store $50 to have it delivered. Friday night another friend and I went out to the Kowloon (a glittery Polynesian restaurant). We were there from 8 until 11:30. We had four pu-pu platters. We ditched the car in Lynn (another city) and went home. They never would have found it; I hid it so good. On Saturday, Tommy and Jimmy, two cops who arrested me before, came to my house. They told me I might as well admit it. They're good cops. I gave them the rest of the money. I told them where the car was.

(He thinks that Gignac saw him in the car and picked him out from a mug book.)

Yanelli: I know all the guards. They like me. (He has been in Charles Street Jail before.) I got to learn my lesson sooner or later. I got to serve time so I don't do this anymore. And tell people to leave their cars locked up and don't leave $10,000 in the car where anybody can get it. He left his wallet in the car, too. This guy is a complete idiot.

(Yanelli tells you he's 22, unemployed, living in East Boston practically his whole life, graduated from Boston Technical High School and is well liked around the neighborhood.)

Yanelli: I can't hold on to a job. I got a temper and a half.

You: Did you have a good time?

Yanelli: Yeah. It was great. I love flashing 100s around. I spent it on true friends, though.

You: What else did you buy?

Yanelli: Watch, clothes, ring, radio, 4 Beatles tapes. If I do time, I want to do it here (Charles Street Jail). I like it here.

He is dressed in a T-shirt, Army fatigue pants and basketball shoes. He says he also bought four pairs of basketball shoes.

The editor tells you to write it in 750 words.

Broadcast News Writing

11

11-1. Simplify words

Broadcast writing depends on clarity and simplicity. One- or two- syllable words are better than those with three or more syllables. Substitute these words for simpler ones.

1. utilize
2. interrogate
3. purchase
4. necessitate
5. deceased
6. terminate
7. contribute
8. perpetrator
9. apprehended
10. incarcerated

11-2. Rewrite sentences in active voice

Good writers try to use strong verbs and active voice in print journalism, but broadcast writing requires active voice even more. Change these sentences into active voice and strengthen the verbs when possible.

Passive: The fire was started by three boys, police said.
Active: Police say three boys started the fire.

1. The food chain owned by Carrs has been purchased by Safeway Inc.
2. Two apartment houses on the east side of town were destroyed by fire this morning.
3. Addiction to the Internet is considered a growing problem among college students by many professors.
4. There are several reasons offered by psychiatrists for the appeal of the Internet to college students.
5. There is an accident at the intersection of Northern Lights Boulevard and Bragaw Street almost every month.
6. At least 30 homes were destroyed in the fire that swept the hillside.
7. There are going to be several students who will have to drop out of school if tuition is increased.
8. An Anchorage man was shot by police after it was discovered that he killed a moose.

44

9. The lottery was won by two students.

10. The getaway car was driven by a perpetrator whom police suspect had been involved in several other robberies.

11-3. Church embezzler

Copy and paste this information into a Word document. Then write a television news story from the following notes. First decide the focus of the story. Then write a lead, either direct or indirect, related to your focus. Write the story as a :20 (20 second) anchor on-camera reader, a story with no video, only the anchor reading on camera. Assume that these locations are in your community or substitute with your cities or towns. Use correct style for broadcast.

A trial has just ended in Johnson County District Court. The defendant, Ron Poteet, 26, 1010 Wellington Road, was caught pocketing monies from the collection plate at Presbyterian Fellowship Church, 2416 Clinton Parkway. Both addresses are in Overland Park (or your city). He was arrested on June 6 of the previous year. He had been entrusted with counting the daily donations and was sentenced earlier today (just after 2 p.m.) to three years in prison. That was his job since 1996.

The pastor of the church, Gordon Price, said yesterday that he had been impressed from the beginning with Poteet's work and thought he was "extremely nice. Polite. Reserved. Gentlehearted. I assumed everything was OK. I was wrong."

Poteet was caught when discrepancies between the amounts entered on the donation envelopes, and the actual amount of money contained inside the envelopes were noticed by another church employee. The investigation was then handed over to the police. In all, about $70,000 was taken by Poteet, although the exact amount isn't known. Price said he debated a long time over whether or not to prosecute.

Poteet was sentenced in courtroom D by Judge Jane Shepherdson to serve 3 years and pay a fine of $10,000. He had pleaded guilty earlier. He made no statement to the court, either when he pleaded or was sentenced.

Exercise written by John Broholm, broadcast journalism professor at the University of Kansas.

11-4. Lumber fire

Write a brief "voiceover" story, a story with accompanying videotape, for this follow-up story. Follow-up stories run a day or more after the event covered to update viewers on recent developments. Your story will run on your station's 6 p.m. evening newscast. The fire happened in a small, nearby community, which received aid from the fire department at another nearby community. Your station was able to obtain videotape of the fire but no interviews from the scene, and your information comes from a wire story. The first sentence of your story will be "on camera," and then the director will go to the videotape.

(DELTON) – Investigators continued to search for the cause of a fire last night that heavily damaged the Delton Lumber Co., while the lumber company's owner worked to get back into business.

45

The blaze was fought by firefighters from Springfield and Delton as part of a mutual aid pact signed by the two cities.

A 4 p.m. meeting was scheduled for today by fire and law enforcement officials from Springfield and Delton at the Springfield/Hamilton County Law Enforcement Center to discuss the fire that destroyed two buildings at the lumberyard and a nearby historic railroad depot, which was used for storage by the lumber company.

No one was injured in the fire that began at approximately 8:30 p.m. in one of the lumber yard buildings, spread to the depot and burned brightly in the night sky until it was brought under control at about 11:00 p.m.

"We're just going to discuss the investigation and where we need to go from here," Springfield Fire Chief Herman McMahon said today.

McMahon said he, Hamilton County Sheriff John Chavez, Delton's acting police chief, Kenny Gault, and Larry Westerman, a Springfield firefighter in charge of the investigation, would be among officials at the meeting.

Dennis Salyer, lumberyard owner, said he hoped to be doing business in a limited way within one or two days, depending on how much the fire episode had disrupted power and lights to the lumberyard office, which suffered only smoke damage.

"We'll do the best we can because we've got some contractor customers who need lumber for building projects," said Salyer.

Officials haven't determined the cause of the fire, which resulted in at least $200,000 in damage.

An official estimate of the damage is being withheld pending inspection by insurance adjusters, McMahon said.

Exercise written by John Broholm, broadcast journalism professor at the University of Kansas.

11-5. Acid arrests

From the following notes, write a short package news story, with an anchor intro and with your recorded voice delivering the main section of the story. Use one or two sound bites with news sources from the quoted material in the notes. You may substitute the names of your community for the ones in this story.

You have been told by Otto Privette, the regional director of the Drug Enforcement Administration, the arm of the U.S. Justice Department that is concerned with illegal drug trafficking, that the D.E.A., the F.B.I., and local law enforcement agencies in northeastern Kansas have seen a significant hike in arrests for sale and/or use of LSD. All told, there have been 10 arrests since the beginning of the year, up from just three all of last year, according to Privette, and the year still has four months to go. LSD was a popular hallucinogenic, countercultural drug in the 1960s. (Phone calls to local law enforcement offices confirmed Privette's assertion of an increase in arrests.) Privette predicted 10 more arrests during the remainder of the year. Privette said that overall in the Kansas City and Lawrence areas:

"More people are using acid, and we're sure arresting more people these days. It's a good bet we'll make some more arrests because we've got three investigators running down leads full-time. In a way it's discouraging because there's so much of the drug around, but I think we're making some headway on the problem." (:12)

Privette said police in the region were looking to arrest manufacturers, sellers, and users, and they're particularly on the lookout for clues leading to the apprehension of a probable local manufacturer of the drug. Privette said it was common for LSD to be manufactured locally.

Lynne Harris, who works for the state of Kansas as a counselor for juveniles who have been arrested on drug-related offenses, said police were arresting many teenagers on LSD-related offenses. She said the drug was popular with teenagers because it was relatively inexpensive and provided a longer "trip" or high than many other drugs. LSD manufacturers have always added one of many varieties of stimulant to the drug to accelerate its entry into and assimilation by the human metabolism, according to Harris. She said the intended purpose of the stimulant was to enhance the sensation of euphoria, or "rush," caused by the drug. She said she didn't know whether the strychnine contamination was for that purpose, or was simply a byproduct of drug production:

"A lot of the LSD we've been seeing has impurities in it. Now the drug's dangerous enough as it is because it can really unhinge people who are already emotionally unstable. But once you add something like strychnine, you can wind up with some pretty toxic stuff. So it's doubly dangerous." (:10)

Harris guessed that if LSD was in Lawrence, it was also showing up around the rest of the country. He said that it was possible there was a manufacturer in Kansas, but that it took a fairly skilled chemist to make the drug, moreso than for metamphetamines, a manufacturer of which was recently discovered in Kansas City by police. Harris said that there were no local reports of the drug falling into the hands of children in grade school, although she had seen reports from elsewhere of acid-impregnated stamps showing cartoon characters.

You have the following videotape:
- Privette showing you evidence bags containing LSD capsules, shot at Kansas City DEA headquarters (up to :30).
- A group counseling session run in Lawrence by Harris, with six teen-agers who are recovering drug users, whose faces you can't show on camera (up to :20).
- The police testing lab in Kansas City, which determines the chemical makeup of confiscated drugs and material (up to :30).

Exercise written by John Broholm, broadcast journalism professor at the University of Kansas.

11-6. Brief news (Write a 15-second spot)

Write a brief 15-second spot (about five lines) based on this press release:

The Justice Club at (your university) will sponsor "Bringing Human Rights Home," on Tuesday, November 10 from 6 to 8:30 p.m. in Arts Building Room 150. Following a short documentary film featuring death row prisoner George McFarland and immigrant Jesus Collado, there will be a panel discussion with four panelists, and an open forum with the audience."Bringing Human Rights Home" will focus on the topics of the death penalty, immigrants' rights, prisoners' rights and habeas corpus relief. Speakers include Rich Curtner, Federal Defender for the state, and Robin Bronen, Director of Immigration and Refugee Services (Catholic Social Services Program).

47

Online Journalism 12

12-1. Plan an online news site

Plan an online news site for your campus or community. If you already have one, plan how you might improve it or develop a competing online site. Working individually or in small groups, brainstorm the kinds of stories and online features you would include in your publication. If you are working in groups, divide the responsibilities for sections in your newspaper. For example, you could have the following editors: city editor responsible for local news, sports editor, business editor, national/foreign news editor and a lifestyle/entertainment editor. What interactive elements would you include such as forums, chats, games, discussion questions? What social media links will you include? Then write a plan explaining your concepts. Consider the following questions:

- What features in your online publication would differ from a print publication?
- What kinds of stories or interactive features would appeal to the demographic groups in your market? Are there special groups you would try to reach, such as high school students? Would you include more news of interest to women and minorities, and if so, what kinds of stories would you suggest?
- Don't forget to brainstorm the interactive features you would include.
- What topics would lend themselves to reader participation and social media?

12-2. Multimedia package

Assume that you are planning a Web package for your campus newspaper or magazine. Using any of the topics suggested here or one you prefer, plan a multimedia storyboard for your package. Include links and interactive elements. You can also include multimedia elements. Be as creative as you wish. This is just a planning exercise; you don't have to produce this package. Some suggested topics:

- Increase in plagiarism on the Internet
- Binge drinking on college campuses
- Tuition increases at your university (with national comparisons)
- Campus crime (also consider national comparisons)
- Spring Break or any upcoming holiday
- Any topic of interest on your campus or in your community

48

12-3. Analyze college news sites

Compare and critique six college news websites. Choose three good ones and three that you think are bad sites. You can start with Campus Grotto, which lists 10 of the best college sites, which include the *Yale Daily News*, the University of Arizona *Daily Wildcat* and the University of North Carolina's *Daily Tar Heel* at the top. Then choose any three college news sites that you don't like. Write an analysis explaining the qualities of good and bad sites. Consider some of these factors in your critique:

- Navigation
- Download time
- Multimedia
- Quality of news
- Blogs and social media
- Appearance
- Special features

12-4. Headlines and blurbs for Web and mobile media

Good headlines on the Web and for mobile media are crucial because readers often have more competition for their attention on the Web than in print publications. Also because of the space limitations of mobile media, enticing headlines are crucial. Headlines should reveal the main idea of the story. A brief headline of fewer than six to eight words is preferable to one that will span two lines.

Write headlines and blurbs for the following information; consider that your headline might stand alone on a Web page without the benefit of the blurb. Your blurb should be the lead you would create for the story or the nut graph.

a. A Harvard University professor disappeared more than a month ago. Yesterday (use the day of the week) his body was found in the Mississippi River at Vidalia, La. The body of Don Wiley, 57, was discovered snagged on a tree near a hydroelectric plant. His abandoned rental car had been found a few weeks earlier on a Mississippi River bridge at Memphis, Tenn., about 300 miles north of Vidalia. A wallet containing his identification was found on the body. Police said no evidence of foul play was found in the car.

b. A custodian at the Halliday, N.D., Public School District has become the head of the high school's science department. Ned Atkin started his first day at the rural school in western North Dakota wearing coveralls and boots, much like his uniform as the former custodian. "I didn't know if I was officially the janitor or a teacher that first morning I came in," he said. His promotion was due to an unexpected resignation of the district's only science teacher. Atkin has a degree in animal science.

49

c. The North Bend (Wash.) City Council passed an "inattentive drivers" ordinance yesterday to target people who violate traffic laws because they were distracted by eating, smoking, reading or talking on cell phones. It will also apply to people who put on makeup or otherwise don't watch the roads. The law takes effect Jan. 1 in this town about 30 miles east of Seattle. Police can already cite motorists for negligent driving, but this new ordinance spells out specific activities that could lead to fines.

d. They're blaming it on loose laws and a cowboy culture. Whatever the cause, the facts are that people on Montana's roads are more likely to die in alcohol-related crashes than motorists in any other state except Mississippi. Montana ranks second in the nation as the highest rate of alcohol-related traffic deaths. Montana has resisted lowering the legal blood-alcohol rate from 0.10 percent to .08 percent as more than half of the other states in the country have done. And Montana allows open alcoholic-beverage containers in vehicles outside cities. That means drivers can have a beer or other alcoholic drink while they drive on the highways.

e. A new website has been created for kittens and cats. The site is geared to cats that are fascinated with moving objects. The site gives cats a choice of three objects to chase: a bird, a bee and a butterfly, each with sounds such as a chirping sound for the bird, a buzzing sound for the bee and a whirring sound for the butterfly. Steve Malarkey, the site designer, said many cats like to chase the cursor on computer screens, so this is just an alternative. The site is www.catty.com.

12-5. Web briefs

Readers using smart phones and the Web want their information in many forms – headline only, summary blurb, briefs, full story or extended information. For a news story, you might just summarize the first few paragraphs. Write these stories as complete briefs, preferably with a catchy ending. Write the briefs as directed – some are only a sentence or two while others are a few paragraphs.

a. Write a brief of one or two sentences based on the following information:

A Colorado State University professor of environmental health has studied the lifestyles of 51 dogs with lung cancer. John Reif, the researcher, found that dogs with short noses are 50 percent more likely to develop lung cancer when they live with owners who smoke. The researchers also studied 83 dogs with other forms of cancer. Reif is using the dogs as models to study the environmental effects of smoke on human beings. He said the study confirms findings that exposure to environmental tobacco smoke increases the risk of human lung cancer. Reif found that long-nosed dogs, such as collies and retrievers, seemed to be protected against passive smoke. The study appeared in the American Journal of Epidemiology. Reif is also studying the effects of pesticides on dogs.

b. Write a two-paragraph brief based on the following information.

A University of South Florida professor is operating the country's first solar-powered vehicle. Professor Lee Stefanakos is chairman of USF's electrical engineering department. He is operating the vehicle at the university's Tampa campus, which is the test site for a fleet of 12 electric vans, cars and trucks. The vehicles get their energy from the sun. The vehicles have solar panels mounted in a carport roof. The solar-powered cars come equipped with air conditioning and other options. The vehicles cover up to 60 miles on a charge and can reach speeds up to 55 miles per hour. The cost of operating the vehicles is about 4 cents per mile. The cost of operating a gasoline-powered car is about 40 cents a mile. The solar-powered cars have 36 batteries mounted under the vehicle. They weigh a total of 1,200 pounds. "Florida does not have any energy resource of its own except the sun, so it makes sense to use it," Stefanakos said. The university received a $1 million grant from the U.S. Department of Energy to study ways to make motorists less dependent on gasoline.

Based on a story from the *Sun-Sentinel*, (Fort Lauderdale, Fla.) Used with permission.

12-6. Chunk-style writing with cliffhangers

Some online readers prefer chunk-style stories that span several pages with each page contained on one or two screens and links at the bottom that entice the readers to continue. Those links or the last sentence of the chunk should be written as a cliffhanger – a sentence or paragraph that provides some mystery. Write this story in chunk style with cliffhangers at the end of each chunk. Limit your story to about three chunks with each chunk no more than one or two screens. Here is the information, which is not well worded or in good order:

The event took place at National Furniture Liquidators at 1202 Maple Grove Road.

A skunk wandered through the open door of the store on Monday afternoon. Throughout the day, store employees tried to catch it. By 8 p.m. the store closed and the skunk was still at large. Efforts to capture it had failed.

The store has thousands of dollars worth of overstuffed chairs, sofas and loveseats. When the skunk first walked in, Dennis Goke, acting assistant manager, wasn't taking any chances. So for the first hour, the skunk was allowed run of the place. It wandered up and down warehouse aisles while employees eyeballed it warily from the doorway. As customers pulled into the parking lot, they were greeted by the unsettling warning of "Hey, we got a loose skunk in here!"

Originally when the skunk walked in three employees did what anyone would do. They hid. Through the rest of the day, although the employees stayed outside more than in, the store didn't close. Business continued throughout the afternoon, if not exactly business as usual.

"If it would have been a squirrel, I would have chased him out with a broom," Goke said.

At one point, the employees tried to lure it out with a trail of whole wheat bread crumbs, but the skunk wasn't hungry. However, the crumbs attracted dozens of gulls, who screeched and screamed and flapped and gorged until most of the bread was gone.

51

"I've worked in strange situations before," Goke said. "I've worked in floods. I've worked without any power in the building." But none of those circumstances had the opportunity to wreak as much havoc as a skunk.

Store manager Bill Frolichman, who had been on vacation, arrived late in the afternoon to oversee the situation. He decided to wait until closing, then tried to spook out the skunk with bright lights and rock music.

Earlier in the day, after the attempts by employees to lure the skunk out failed, Rich Ulkus of Animal Allies arrived to see what he could do. By then the skunk had had enough. There were too many people around and too much commotion. It disappeared into hiding somewhere in the bowels of the store.

That made employees more nervous than watching it roam the aisles.

Ulkus spent a few minutes on his hands and knees, shining a floodlight under some of the couches and drawing gasps of admiration and comments about his bravery from the others, but he couldn't find the skunk, so he and Goke baited a trap with tuna, wrapped the tuna in several layers of plastic, then wrapped the whole thing in a blanket and stuck it in a corner.

Based on a story from *The* (Duluth, Minn.) *News-Tribune*. Used with permission.

12-7. Web news story

Web experts mentioned in your textbook recommend writing online stories with boldfaced subheads, lists and inverted pyramid style to help readers scan material. Although those recommendations don't need to apply to all stories, they are helpful for many basic news stories. Use those techniques to write this story based on a press release from the U.S. Department of Commerce. Add a headline and summary blurb. Write short paragraphs and condense this story to about one computer screen, depending on the margins. If you want to add more quotes, consider interviewing some of your classmates or other students about their views or experiences of sexual victimization on campus.

The U.S. Department of Justice's National Institute of Justice and the Bureau of Justice Statistics released a report today. The report, "The Sexual Victimization of College Women," offers a comprehensive look into the prevalence and nature of sexual assault occurring at American colleges. The federally funded study was conducted by Bonnie S. Fisher, a professor at the University of Cincinnati, Francis T. Cullen and Michael G. Turner.

The study showed that about 3 percent of college women experience a completed and/or attempted rape during a college year. The data show that about 1.7 percent of female college students were victims of attempted rape. About 1.7 percent of the college women reported being coerced to have sex. The study also estimated that about 13 percent of college women have been stalked since the beginning of the school year. Of the incidents of sexual victimization, the vast majority occurred after 6 p.m. in living quarters. For completed rapes, nearly 60 percent that took place on campus occurred in the victim's residence, 31 percent occurred in other living quarters on campus and 10 percent occurred at a fraternity. Most off-campus victimization, especially rapes, also

52

occurred in residences. However, particularly for sexual contacts and threatened victimizations, incidents also took place in bars, dance clubs, nightclubs and work settings.

"Most victims knew the person who sexually victimized them," the authors wrote. "For both completed and attempted rapes, about nine in 10 offenders were known to the victim. Most often, a boyfriend, ex-boyfriend, classmate, friend acquaintance, or coworker sexually victimized the women. College professors were not identified as committing any rapes or sexual coercions, but they were cited as the offender in a low percentage of cases involving unwanted sexual contact."

The National Institute of Justice and the Bureau of Justice Statistics are components of the Office of Justice Programs, which also includes the Bureau of Justice Assistance, the Office of Juvenile Justice and Delinquency Prevention, and the Office for Victims of Crime.

Based on their findings, Bonnie Fisher and her colleagues estimate that the women at a college that has 10,000 female students could experience more than 350 rapes a year--a finding with serious policy implications for college administrators. Fisher also found that many women do not characterize their sexual victimizations as a crime for a number of reasons (such as embarrassment, not clearly understanding the legal definition of rape or not wanting to define someone they know who victimized them as a rapist) or because they blame themselves for their sexual assault. The study reinforces the importance of many organizations' efforts to improve education and knowledge about sexual assault.

Attention to the sexual victimization of college women, however, also has been prompted by the rising fear that college campuses are not ivory towers but, instead, have become hot spots for criminal activity. Researchers have shown that college campuses and their students are not free from the risk of criminal victimization. Previous research suggests that these women are at greater risk for rape and other forms of sexual assault than women in the general population or in a comparable age group. College women might, therefore, be a group whose victimization warrants special attention.

Who was surveyed?

NCWSV study results are based on a telephone survey of a randomly selected, national sample of 4,446 women who were attending a 2- or 4-year college or university. The sample was limited to schools with at least 1,000 students. Furthermore, from a policy perspective, college administrators might be disturbed to learn that for every 1,000 women attending their institutions, there may well be 35 incidents of rape in a given academic year (based on a victimization rate of 35.3 per 1,000 college women). For a campus with 10,000 women, this would mean the number of rapes could exceed 350. Even more broadly, when projected over the Nation's female student population of several million, these figures suggest that rape victimization is a potential problem of large proportion and of public policy interest.

12-8. Mobile media version

iPads, other tablet computers and smart phones are affecting the way online journalism should be written. Although tablet computers can display stories in the same formats as a print publication, competition for the reader's attention is great because of the multitude of applications, social media links and other diversions. Brief stories may be better on small screens. Rewrite the previous story for mobile media, adding social media links that you think would add value to the content.

Public Relations Writing **13**

The following exercises will give you a chance to do some critical thinking about news releases, media kits and chances to create your own **public** relations materials. Check the CourseMate for this book for online resources that offer many helpful hints on writing press releases and media kits: *http://www.cengagebrain.com.*

13-1. Rewrite a news release

This news release about an event is poorly written and is not in proper form. It also has style errors. Rewrite this release using proper form (name of organization, address, your name as contact and your telephone number and e-mail address); date the release, write a headline and write "FOR IMMEDIATE RELEASE" on the left or above the headline. Double-space the release and type – 30 – at the end. Write one or two paragraphs and eliminate extraneous information.

News Release
To whom it may concern:

Big Brothers/Big Sisters of Douglas County, Inc. will host an informational meeting for prospective volunteers at 10:00 a.m., Saturday, (add Saturday's date). We would be so happy to have you attend, and we would welcome news coverage. The meeting will be at the organization's office at 220 Main st. in Lawrence, 04040. The meeting will last approximately 2 hours and officers of Big Brothers/Big Sisters will discuss how you can become a volunteer to a child who needs adult companionship, which is the purpose of the organization. If you would like more information, call 454-1222 anytime during the week. We are hoping to gain more volunteers for the organization, and will appreciate anything you can do to help us.

I am George Hand, contact for the organization, and I would be happy to talk with you about it. You can call me at the organization's office, 454-1222.

P.S. If anyone can't make this meeting, another informational meeting is scheduled <u>for Tuesday,</u> <u>[add Tuesday's date].</u> That will be at 6:00 p.m.

13-2. Qualities of news releases

Write the answers in your computer, and print out the page.

1. List three qualities of news that your press releases should have for print publications.
2. List three qualities of news that your press releases should have for broadcast (TV).
3. List three qualities of news that your Web releases should have. How would a Web press release differ from print releases?
4. List crucial contact information that all press releases should contain.
5. Make a template (a form) for a print press release. Use the form in your textbook as a guide.
7. Make a template for a fax press release.
8. Compare news releases on three university websites. You can and should check your own college website if you have one. If not, choose your favorite colleges or universities and check out their Web news releases. You can link to them from Yahoo! *http://www.yahoo.com* and search for college and universities or *http://dir.yahoo.com/Education/Higher_Education/Colleges_and_Universities.*
9. Discussion:
   • How do they differ?
   • Which do you like?
   • Which are most helpful?
   • Which would you use if you were an editor at a newspaper?
   • Which would you use if you were a news director at a TV station?
   • How do they differ from a news or feature story you have been taught to write?
10. Now study a corporate public relations wire service. Click into:
   http://www.prnewswire.com or *http://www.businesswire.com.*
   Study a feature package.
   Study a news release from a corporation.
   Discuss the differences.

13-3. Gather information and write news releases

Check information from bulletin boards in your school. Gather information for three events for which you will write press releases.

1. Write one version for print via e-mail.
2. Write another version for broadcast.
3. Write another version for the Web.
4. Write another version for social media.

13-4. News release

Assume this is a news release issued by the Office of University Relations at your university, which has a total enrollment of 24,500 students. Use a hard-news lead and write it in inverted pyramid style. Limit it to one page. Write a headline and use standard press release form. Label it "NEWS RELEASE" and put the University and contact information at the top; use your phone number and e-mail address. You may use today's date and "FOR IMMEDIATE RELEASE." Consider a chart or list format for some of the statistics. Here is the information, which is poorly written.

The university has released figures for its minority enrollment for this fall. The enrollment categories are based on self-reported student data. The minority enrollment has increased. In fact, it increased 8.7 percent this fall. This increase came in a year when overall campus enrollment grew less than 1 percent.

"This university has taken a significant step forward," said [Use the name of your university president or chancellor]. "Our many efforts of recent years are beginning to produce the desired results."

Enrollment of black students increased by 34 students to 678.

"The increase in minority students is a gratifying sight for the many students, faculty and administrators who have worked for it," the chancellor (use his or her name) said. "We still have more to do. This is only the beginning."

In other categories, American Indian student enrollment showed the largest increase of 46 students to a total of 204. Asian student enrollment increased by 44 to 565. Hispanic enrollment grew by 28 to 452.

Comparing minority enrollment for previous years, the statistics show that minority enrollment for five years ago was 1,540 compared to 1,747 last year and 1,899 this year.

13-5. Web news release

Using the following information, write a news release for the Web. Instead of double-spacing, as in print releases, use single spacing, and insert a space between paragraphs. Be sure to include relevant URLs for the company. You may use a hard-news or feature approach. Limit your release to no more than two screens, preferably one screen. Put a posting date at the end of your document. Use proper AP style. (You might want to check out the site before you write your release.)

Headline: This is about offering free greeting cards with astrological messages
Press Contact: You (and your phone numbers and e-mail address)
The company name is **Access: NewAge.** The Web site address is
http://www.accessnewage.com.

Here is the information:

The company prides itself on being a major link to the spiritual and New Age community. Access: NewAge is expanding its services by offering free online personalized astrological greeting cards. For example: Happy Birthday, Sagittarian . . . or Libra . . . or Gemini. Or possibly Congratulations Pisces. I love you Taurus. Good luck Leo. These are some examples.

You can now send friends, lovers, and family free astrological greeting cards courtesy of Access: NewAge.

Our website address is *http://www.accessnewage.com.*

Each card contains an astrological profile and a link to an up-to-date monthly horoscope for the sign. Senders can send their greeting with any message and choose a special background. If they know HTML, they can code the greeting card effects.

Bob Siegel, webmaster of the company's website (www.accessewAge.com) says, "Access: NewAge was created with the intent of offering content on all things esoteric, spiritual and metaphysical. Free customizable astrological greeting cards are the step. And, if visitors want to order a gift to go with the card, like a book or aromatherapy products, they can do that at our site."

The website, *www.accessnewage.com* was launched in 1995 and currently boasts over 30,000 unique visitors a day and provides links to other esoteric, spiritual and new age sites. The site's Looking Deeper Magazine offers visitors hundreds of online articles from some of the top new age specialists in the field and forecasts from our resident astrologer.

Company Name: Access: NewAge

Web address: *http://www.accessnewage.com*

Posted: Today's date.

13-6. Product promotion - print and Web

Write this news release in print form. Then convert it to Web format. Your textbook contains a press release from Crayola LLC to promote new washable crayons. Now the company has come out with another new product – its first highlighters for kids. They, too, are washable. Write a news release to promote this product. Use standard double-space form, and limit your release to one page (approximately three to four paragraphs). Make sure you include the company name, address, telephone number, and use your name as the contact person with your telephone number. Label your release "For Immediate Release." Write a headline at the top of the release, and use Easton, Pa. as your dateline. Here is the information:

The company uses "From Crayola Products" above its name, Crayola LLC., 1100 Church Lane, P.O. Box 431, Easton, Pennsylvania 18044-0431 [use your phone number].

The company was called Binney & Smith, but changed its name Crayola in 2007. It produces Crayola products, which include crayons and markers and paints and a variety of other products. The company is introducing a new line of products, which it says is its first set of highlighters specifically designed for kids.

The product will be called Crayola Screamin' Neons.   These are washable school highlighters that were designed especially for schoolchildren. The products are bright, neon colors. Bright, neon graphics on each highlighter "scream" kids and fun. The highlighters feature a special rounded nib that allows a smooth flow of ink without noise or squeaking. They are washable. The washable formula is patented. It allows the highlighter ink to be washed from hands, face and most children's clothing. They are non-toxic. They are available in a pack of four colors: glowing green, neon yellow, hot magenta and electric blue.

The suggested retail price is $1.99. The highlighters were developed after research conducted by the company revealed that children start using highlighters around the age of 8. The research also revealed that they continue using highlighters throughout their school use. The research also indicated that children use highlighters for a variety of activities. Some of those activities include school papers, study sheets, plays, maps and reports. Tailoring a highlighter to the needs of children resulted in the development of Screamin' Neons.

In addition to the press release information for this product, you are including this background about the company; decide if any of this should go in the press release or should be packaged separately:

Crayola LLC, was founded by C. Harold Smith and Edwin Binney in 1885. Slate pencils and chalk preceded the company's introduction of Crayola crayons in 1903.

Each year the company produces more than 2 billion Crayola crayons.

Tests reveal that the smell of Crayola crayons is one of the 20 most recognizable aromas to American adults. Coffee and peanut butter top the list.

On the average, children ages 2 to 7 color or draw 28 minutes a day.

In a given year, Crayola manufactures enough Crayola paint to cover all of the major league baseball and football stadiums and the Brooklyn Bridge combined.

In addition to crayons, Crayola products include markers, watercolors, tempera paints, chalk, clay, washable paints as well as fabric paints.

Each year American children spent 6.3 billion hours coloring – almost 10,000 human lifetimes.

Crayola crayons are currently sold in more than 60 countries from the island of Iceland to the tiny Central American nation of Belize. Crayola product boxes are printed in 11 different languages including English, Spanish, French, Dutch and Italian.

The first box of Crayola crayons sold for 5 cents.

Based on a news release from Crayola LLC. Used with permission.

13-7. Design a media kit

Choose an organization or topic (upcoming holiday). A local nonprofit organization would be a good client. Design a media kit that includes:
- Press releases about upcoming news.
- Backgrounder about the organization or company.
- Feature story about the organization or company.
- Photos or graphics (or suggestions for either).

- Related Web links for the organization.
- Cover (optional) with creative graphic.

Suggestions for study: Click into a website for a major company or organization such as Hallmark, which is featured in your textbook.

13-8. Critique a corporate or public relations agency website

Choose a company where you might like to have an internship or a job. Write an analysis of its website. Consider some of the following points in your critique:

- Does the site list contact information? Does this information include a physical address and any phone numbers?
- Is the site easy to use?
- Does the site include information about how to apply for job or internships?
- Does the site give clear and interesting information about its products or mission?
- Does the site have good navigation?
- Does the site contain information about social media links?
- Does the site contain good graphics?
- Does the site information load quickly?
- What are the pros and cons of the site?
- What recommendations would you have for the company based on its website?
- If you were applying for an internship at the company, what information would you gain from the site for your interview?

Media Law

14

14-1. Libel quiz #1 – *multiple choice quiz*

1. The textbook has listed four defenses against libel (truth, Sullivan, privilege, fair comment and criticism). From a reporter's point of view, which is the strongest and why?

    a. Truth

    b. Sullivan

    c. Privilege

    d. Fair comment and criticism

2. With respect to libel law, what does "actual malice" mean?

    a. That the reporter was careless

    b. That the reporter tried to be mean to the plaintiff

    c. That the reporter was malicious

    d. That the reporter made a false statement either knowing the information was wrong or with reckless disregard for whether it was wrong

3. The "actual malice" standard comes into play in a libel suit

    a. with private figure plaintiffs who cannot prove negligence.

    b. with plaintiffs who are public officials or public figures.

    c. only when the news organization refuses to print a correction.

    d. only when the news organization sues a public official for libel.

4. Which of the following is *not* a reason the Supreme Court established the "actual malice" test in Sullivan?

    a. To encourage robust debate on public issues

    b. To encourage a free press to publish matters of public concern

    c. In recognition that important public debate may include vehement, caustic and sharp attacks on public officials

    d. In recognition that in a democracy, private figures, too, have to be ready for sharp or unpleasant attacks in the press

5. With respect to libel law, "privilege" means

    a. You can report anything in a public place without worrying about checking facts.

    b. You can go on private property to gather information.

    c. You may print defamatory statements from a public proceeding or public record as long as you are being fair and accurate.

    d. You have the absolute privilege to report the news, guaranteed by the First Amendment.

6. As a news photographer, you use a telephoto lens to shoot pictures in your neighbor's back yard, some 300 feet from your location on a public sidewalk.

    a. You may be guilty of invasion of privacy under the intrusion category.

    b. You are protected from any action because you're a journalist.

    c. Your neighbor can sue you for libel if you print a topless picture of her.

    d. You are protected from an invasion of privacy – public disclosure of private facts action because you've taken the information from a public place, and that is the same as the public record.

7. Your advertising department wants to use a picture of the hometown baseball hero in an automobile dealer advertisement.

    a. Because he's a public figure, the ad people can simply clip a photo from the files and put it in without notifying the hometown hero.

    b. The ad people can use him because he is newsworthy.

    c. The ad people have to receive his permission and pay him if he requests it, since this is for commercial purposes.

    d. This could be considered an invasion of privacy under false light publicity

8. You have been sued for invasion of privacy – public disclosure of private facts – for publishing a person's less-than-flattering mental health history. You will likely win the suit if

    a. you took the information from a public record.

    b. the person's physician said it was OK to use the information.

    c. you print a retraction.

    d. you obtained the document from an anonymous source.

9. With respect to accuracy, experienced journalists

    a. don't worry about it too much since the Sullivan defense is there to protect them.

    b. usually check the major facts, then "go with their gut."

    c. check details, even little things, to see if a source or story "doesn't add up."

    d. know the "corrections" column is there to back them up.

10. Showing your copy to sources before it is published

    a. is never permitted.

    b. is a sign that you doubt the truth of your story.

    c, will lead to a lawsuit.

    d. is a way that some journalists catch inaccuracies before publication.

This exercise was written by Tom Volek, media law professor at the University of Kansas.

14-2. Libel quiz #2 – *essay format*

Using your computer, write brief answers to the following questions:

1. What is the difference between libel and slander?

2. What are the three types of public figures? Define each type.

3. In *Hutchinson v. Proxmire,* on what grounds did the court rule that Hutchinson was not a public figure?

4. If a public official sues a newspaper for libel, what does the official have to prove to the court?

5. How do the standards for proving libel differ for a public official and a private individual in many states?

6. Define absolute privilege.

7. Define qualified privilege.

8. What are the four grounds for invasion of privacy suits?

9. In *Dietemann v. Time Inc.,* why did the court rule in favor of Dietemann?

10. What is the purpose of the Uniform Corrections Act and what type of correction would a publication have to run if it is sued for libel?

14-3. Online legal issues – *True/false quiz*

Answer the following questions by writing true or false.

1. If someone posts a libelous message to an online discussion group without using his or her real name, the Internet service provider is responsible for the liability.
    a. True
    b. False

2. The U.S. Supreme Court ruled that the Communications Decency Act of 1996 could restrict distribution of indecent material on the Internet to people under age 18.
    a. True
    b. False

3. The U.S. Supreme Court ruled that the entire Communications Decency Act of 1996 was unconstitutional.
   a. True
   b. False

4. In *Zeran v. AOL,* the U.S. Supreme Court ruled that America Online was not responsible for the death threats and defamatory messages that Kenneth Zeran received concerning the Oklahoma City bombing of a federal building.
   a. True
   b. False

5. If you take a picture from the Internet from a site that does not have a copyright symbol on it, the information is copyright-free.
   a. True
   b. False

6. If you post a home page on the Internet without using a copyright symbol, you are protected by the U.S. copyright laws.
   a. True
   b. False

7. The No Electronic Theft Act allows you to copy software and online materials as long as you don't make a profit.
   a. True
   b. False

8. If a site is encrypted, that means it contains special codes that only government agents can read.
   a. True
   b. False

9. If you post defamatory material on your site that you selected from other blogs, the courts have ruled that you are responsible.
   a. True
   b. False

10. You can post any type of message on a discussion even if it is libelous because online discussion groups do not qualify as "publication" under the standards applied to libel cases.
   a. True
   b. False

14-4. Legal scenarios – *essay format*

Write the answers or your opinions for these scenarios; if your instructor prefers, discuss them in class. In your discussion or written answers, cite the legal reason.

1. You are at a school board meeting. A member of the audience says the high school guidance counselor has had sex with his students. The remarks are made during the public comment portion of the meeting. Do you publish the comments? If you do, could you be sued for libel?

2. A police officer tells you that a suspect, John W. Sleaze, is a rapist. You publish the officer's comments. Are they libelous?

3. A city council member tells you after a meeting that the council chairman has been accepting bribes in return for his votes on an issue. If you publish his comments, could the council chairman sue you for libel? Does this council member have absolute privilege in this case?

4. You are reviewing a restaurant and you say that roaches crawled across the table. Can the restaurateur sue you for libel?

5. You are reviewing the same restaurant and this time you say that the food was tasteless. Do you have the right to say this without fear of libel?

6. You are on private property and you take a photo of man beating his wife in his house. You are using a telephoto lens and observe this incident, which you see through the window of his house. Is this an invasion of privacy?

7. A nurse at a home for the elderly gives you medical records of patients to prove that some patients were given incorrect medication for their conditions. Can you use these records, using the patients' names? Is this an invasion of privacy?

8. You are planning a campaign for Nike and you use a photograph of Michael Jordan wearing Nike shoes. Can he sue you?

9. You are writing a story about seasonal affective disorder for The Northern Light and you copy comments from a Web site about this disease without attributing them. Is this plagiarism? Is it "fair use"?

10. In a discussion group hosted by the Internet service provider, MSN.com, someone posts an anonymous message that libels you. Can you sue MSN?

Media Ethics

15

15-1. The bad joke – *Choose a or b*

Your reporter is covering a speech by a local politician. The politician makes a joke in the speech that offends several members of the audience, who stand up and walk out. The person covering the speech reports this, but in the story repeats the joke told by the politician. It has a sexual theme. In editing the story:

a. You delete the joke because you consider it offensive and inappropriate for your newspaper.

b. You let it stand on the grounds that otherwise your readers (or viewers) can't properly judge the actions of the politician and those people who walked out.

Case from *The Hartford* (Conn.) *Courant.* Reprinted with permission.

15-2. The telephone number – *Choose a or b*

Your newspaper is about to publish a wire-service story about the "Overground Railroad," a network that would help women get abortions if *Roe v. Wade* were to be overturned. The story is neutral as to whether the right to an abortion should exist, but it includes, at the end, the toll-free number for the Overground Railroad headquarters. In editing the story:

a. You let the phone number stand. You reason that it's simply a way to help interested readers, similar to printing the opening hours of an art exhibit. It's not free advertising, you argue, nor does it promote abortion.

b. You delete the phone number. If the subject were non-controversial, you wouldn't object to providing this information. But the story deals with abortion, one of the most hotly debated issues of the day. And besides, other stories haven't had the phone number for groups like Operation Rescue.

Case from *The Hartford* (Conn.) *Courant.* Reprinted with permission.

15-3. Son of superintendent – *Choose a or b*

A 20-year-old man in your city is arrested on morals charges involving a 17-year-old girl. Your reporter writes the story, and it includes the fact that the arrested person is the son of the superintendent of schools. In editing it:

a. You leave in the mention of the father, because you believe this fact is important to readers. The father is well known locally, and such unpleasant publicity is one of the prices of fame. Also, you don't want to be accused of covering up anything touching on a public official.
b. You delete the reference to the father. He is in no way connected to the arrest, and you reason that to report the family connection would be unfair.

Case from *The Hartford* (Conn.) *Courant.* Reprinted with permission.

15-4. A hero's private life

Imagine that you are the editor of your newspaper. Write your justification for the following ethical dilemma as though you had to explain it to your readers (or viewers) in a column on the editorial page or next to the story.

A woman armed with a gun takes aim at the president, but a man intervenes by deflecting her arm. Later, after the newspapers report the news incident, a newspaper writes about the man and identifies him as gay. He had not revealed his sexual preference to his family, and he is upset by this revelation. However, he has become a national hero. As the editor of the newspaper, would you have printed this information about his personal life? Justify your decision.

15-5. Anonymous sources

Your textbook describes an ethical dilemma the editors at the *Seattle Times* faced when eight women accused former U.S. Sen. Brock Adams of sexual harassment. The women refused to allow their names to be used. The senator was running for re-election. Would you have printed the story using anonymous sources? Justify your decision. Write your views in a column, just as Michael Fancher, editor of the Seattle newspaper, did when he published this story.

15-6. Cooperating with police

You are the police reporter for your local newspaper. Police have informed you that they plan to make a sweep of arrests for prostitution at a local park. They ask you to publish the names of the persons they arrest, including the men who solicit the prostitutes. They say that prostitution is a major problem in your community and by publishing the names of the "johns," you can help deter this crime. Your newspaper normally does not publish the names of persons arrested on minor morals charges. What are the ethical problems this case presents? Will you publish the names? Justify your decision by writing pros and cons and discussing harms versus benefits.

15-7. Personal dilemma

Study the ethical guidelines in your textbook. Discuss a personal dilemma you have had either on an internship or during the course of your education. Would you make the same decision now, after using ethical guidelines, as you did at the time?

15-8. Code of ethics

Working in groups, create a code of ethics for your campus newspaper. Check the codes of ethics of journalism organizations by linking to them from the Web site for this book. Devise your own code using some of these topics:
- Use of deception
- Accepting gifts or free tickets
- Anonymous sources
- Altering photographs
- Conflicts of interest – socializing with sources.
- Plagiarism and fabrication

15-9. Online and social media ethical issues

Discuss new ethical dilemmas that are being creating by online and social media, such as the following:
- Would you or should you quote sources from blogs without their permission?
- Would you quote sources from Twitter and Facebook without their permission?
- Should you include links to online plagiarism sites in news stories about the problems of plagiarism on the Internet because of easy access to so much information?
- Should you link to pornographic sites in a news story about the proliferation and popularity of such sites on the Internet? Does it make a difference if your publication is on a university server or is a campus online newspaper or magazine?
- Should you include e-mail messages posted to discussion lists in news stories?
- How would you handle a case of a reporter who lifted information from another source from online sources without permission? Is that plagiarism?

Multicultural Sensitivity

16

16-1. Media survey

If your instructor prefers, you may do this as a class project with each student assigned to a different organization.

Part 1: Conduct a survey of the media in your community and/or state (newspapers, magazines, television stations, advertising and public relations firms) to determine the number of minorities and women in various positions. How many minorities do these organizations employ in news/editorial positions? How many of these minorities or women are in management positions (as editors, for example)? How many minorities or women are in top management positions – managing editors, executive editors, news directors, publishers, and so on? How does this percentage or figure compare with the total number of minorities in the organization, and what types of jobs do the majority of minorities have?

Part 2: Interview top editors of these organizations and ask them if they have any official policies regarding recruiting and hiring of minorities and women in general staff positions and in management positions. Ask editors (or top officials) to explain any efforts they have taken to increase minority representation at their organizations. If they say they are looking for qualified minorities and women, ask them to explain their definition of "qualified."

16-2. Photo sensitivity

Many studies and articles criticize the media for using photographs that portray minorities in a negative or stereotypical light, such as photos portraying African-Americans in crime scenes or only on sports pages. Analyze the photographs or images of minorities – particularly African-Americans, Hispanic-Americans, Asian-Americans or Native Americans – in your local newspaper or other newspapers or on television for a week or more. Or watch television for a week and analyze how minorities are portrayed in the TV news or in advertisements. Do they perpetuate stereotypes? Write an analysis of your findings using the name of the organization (print or broadcast), the date of the issue and a brief description of the situation in which minorities were portrayed.

16-3. Gender stereotypes

Analyze how men and women are portrayed in commercials on television. Be on the lookout for male bashing as much as for female stereotyping. Write the name of the advertiser, a brief description and whether or not you believe the advertisement portrays men and women in stereotypical or sexist ways. If possible, watch the ads with a person of the opposite sex to compare your perceptions. Here are some qualities to look for:

- Are women portrayed in commercials set in the kitchen more than men? Are men being portrayed as inferior to make women look strong, intelligent or superior?
- Are women being used as sex symbols in commercials for products unrelated to physical appearance such as automobile ads or beer ads?
- In commercials about physical appearance such as dieting, are more women featured than men?
- What stereotypes do you think these commercials perpetuate?
- How many of the commercials feature men and women of different races and what types of commercials are they?

Profiles and Obituaries **17**

17-1. Profile checklist

Instructions: Use the questions below as a profile checklist. Answer the following questions in the fields below.

Question 1: Why is this person newsworthy? What has this person done that would be of interest to readers of your college newspaper, Web site or local publication?

Question 2: What will be your focus of the profile?

Question 3: Have you done background research? If so, what are the most interesting and important facts you have uncovered either from a resume or the Internet?

Question 4: What questions have you prepared? List at least five of them here.

Question 5: Who are your other sources that you have contacted or plan to contact?

17-2. Autobiographical profile

If you are applying for a job or for graduate school, you are often asked to write an autobiographical essay.

Using the third-person voice, write a profile about yourself as though you were a stranger. You may add quotes as necessary. Try to show yourself in action by describing some of your idiosyncrasies, habits and the things you do often. Set the scene for your profile and put yourself in it. Add background information as necessary to help the reader understand you and how you got to this point in your life. Although the newsworthy angle and focus are strained, you could imagine that this will be part of a series of profiles or vignettes for a yearbook or a newspaper article about faces on campus. Here is some information you should include before you write the profile:

Part 1- Facts box: First write a facts box and fill in the answers about yourself.
    Favorite books:
    Favorite movies:
    Favorite song:
    Best advice I ever received:

Heroes or heroines:
I chose my current field of study or career because:
One of the hardest decisions I had to make was:
If I could be anything I wanted, I'd be:
My favorite childhood memory is:
I would describe myself as (list character traits):
My friends would describe me as:
When I graduate, I'd like to (go, do, be):
If I could change something about myself, it would be:
The main obstacles I have faced or am facing are:
Add any other questions you think might be helpful.

Part 2 – Description: Write a description of your room, emphasizing items that are meaningful to you. Describe pictures on your wall, specific books, magazines, stuffed animals or anything that characterizes your environment. Imagine that you are interviewing someone else and you are observing his or her environment. Just jot down items if you prefer.

Part 3 – Analysis: Looking at the information you have compiled, analyze it for any patterns or any specific details that reflect your personality. Imagine that these are notes you have taken from an interview with a source.

Here are some questions to ask yourself as you analyze your notes:
• What have I learned or observed about myself that surprises me?
• What one dominant impression do I give, based on the information I have compiled?
• What impression would I like people to have of me?
• Are there any patterns I observe in this information?
• Was there a turning point in my life that made me decide to go to this college or choose my current career field?
• What details about me stand out most?

Part 4 - Write the profile.

17-3. Slice-of-life profile

You are interviewing a mail carrier for a slice-of-life profile about people who work in your community. This person isn't very quotable and she doesn't consider her job extraordinary. But you have to find something interesting for your lead. Consider an anecdotal lead or a show-in-action lead. Using these notes, which are not in good order, write a brief profile:

The letter carrier is Nancy Workman. She has worked for the U.S. Postal Service for five and a half years. Her walking route covers approximately 23 square miles. She spends between four and four and a half hours each day delivering the mail. "I come in each morning at 7:15 a.m., and I sort the mail for about three hours. Then I deliver the mail, and after that, I work at the office, preparing for the next day until 3:15 p.m. Letter carriers choose their own delivery routes based on seniority. I love meeting the people on my route and getting to know them. I chose my route because it was a flat walking route. Most letter carriers prefer driving routes, but driving just never appealed to me. Walking is tremendous medicine, as it's a great time for reflection."

She said winter was the most difficult time to deliver the mail, not only because of the weather, but because she encounters fewer people to talk to. Workman estimates that she walks almost 12 miles each day. Consequently, she closely monitors weather forecasts. "Once you're out there, you have no shelter. There's no place you can hide. The worst thing is sitting at home, worrying the night before a major storm. I have problems sleeping on those nights, just thinking about the coming storm. I love the outdoors, and I love the freedom of the street." Encounters with dogs are a minor job hazard. She carries dog mace in her dusty blue mailbag. "I've only had a dog bite me once, and it was very minor, more like a mosquito bite," Workman said. "Dog poop, though, can really ruin your day."

Workman said she enjoys the unpredictability she faces in the weather and in other aspects of her job. "Each day I come in, and I have no idea how much mail there will be," Workman said. "Some days catalogs are the enemy. Lately, Victoria's Secret has been just crazy — sending out new catalogs all the time." Workman plans to remain a letter carrier indefinitely. "I really do love this job," she said. "I plan to keep delivering the mail until I can't walk anymore." The most unusual experience she had was when one of her patrons failed to pick up his mail for several days. "His mail just kept piling up, and after a while, it worried me. I didn't want to overreact. But then I noticed the front door of his house. His screen door was covered with flies. I went next door and asked the man's neighbors to call the police. The police discovered that the middle-aged man had died of a heart attack several days ago. I was hoping I was wrong, but I had a really eerie feeling about the whole situation. It was really scary because I knew this man, and suddenly he was dead."

17-4. Obituaries

These exercises will give you practice writing standard-form obituaries and feature obituaries. Use the examples in your textbook as models. Include the cause of death and courtesy titles, even though many newspapers may not require either. Use Associated Press style, not the style in the death notices, which are often written and paid for by the family or funeral home and do not follow newspaper style. Omit the flowery language and euphemisms. People die. They don't "enter into rest," "depart," or "pass away." Write the obituaries as directed.

a. Write this obituary in standard form with courtesy titles for the person who died, male or female. This information is adapted from an obituary published in *The Oregonian*, but the name of the deceased and addresses have been changed.

Samuel Morris Burnside, beloved father of Harold G. of Salem and Dr. Robert M. of Springfield; devoted grandfather of 10 grandchildren, eight great-grandchildren; and two great-great-grandchildren, passed away Monday. He was a retired real estate broker and past president and lieutenant governor of Division 64 of Kiwanis Pacific Northwest District. Funeral services, 1 p.m. Friday in the chapel of Young's Funeral Home, 640 Broad St., in Tigard. Burial in Crescent Grove Cemetery, 320 Main St., Portland. The family suggests remembrances be contributions to Southwest Hills Kiwanis Club.

You call the funeral home and the family and get this additional information:

He was born April 29, 1920. The family says the cause of death is heart failure. He died in the Portland Care Center in Southwest Portland where he had resided for the past 10 years. He was born in Weber, Utah, and grew up on a farm near Grant, Idaho. He moved to Portland from Jerome, Idaho, in 1942.

He attended the University of Idaho and Albin State Normal School. He retired many years ago but had worked as a real estate broker in the Southwest Portland area for many years.

He was past president and lieutenant governor of Division 64 of Kiwanis Pacific Northwest District. Survivors include his sons, Harold G. of Salem and Dr. Robert M. of Springfield; 10 grandchildren, eight great-grandchildren; and two great-great-grandchildren.

Based on an obituary from *The Oregonian*. Used with permission.

b. Your editor wants you to advance this obituary by starting with the funeral arrangements because the person died five days earlier. Use courtesy titles for the deceased and cause of death. Be sure to follow Associated Press style, not the style in the following death notice from the funeral home. Note AP style for states, not Postal Service style. Use the simpler word "burial" instead of "interment."

Sandra K. Sullivan, beloved daughter of Zoe Margolis, loving mother of sons, Christopher and Vernon of [your town] and Archie of Lansing, MI.; and daughter Mattie Hills of San Francisco, CA., died Saturday. Leaves numerous nieces and nephews. She was born June 12, 1950. A native of (your town) and lifelong resident, she devoted herself to helping others. Friends are welcome for Visitation Friday from 9 A.M. to 9 P.M. and are respectfully invited to attend Funeral Services Saturday at 10 A.M. in the St. Paul's Baptist Church, 9030 Addison Place, [Your town]. Private interment. Remembrances may be made to the Sandra K. Sullivan musical scholarships at the church.

You call the family and funeral home. You notice that Sandra Sullivan is survived by her mother and children, but there is no mention of a husband in the death notice. You ask how she would prefer to be addressed, and her family tells you to use "Ms." Other information from the family and funeral home includes:

Cause of death – cancer. She died in her home.

Occupation: She was director of the private Foundation for Independent Living in your town, an organization that helps disabled people. She worked for the organization for 20 years and was director for the past 10 years. She was also an accomplished pianist and choir musical director for St. Paul's Baptist Church. She graduated from the high school in your town and earned a bachelor's degree in social work from Michigan State University and a master's degree in social work from New York University.

She was divorced in 1980 from Harry G. Sullivan, but her family says they do not want that mentioned in the obituary.

c. This information is also from a paid death notice. You supplement it with interviews from the family. Use courtesy titles and cause of death. Make sure you check AP style for abbreviations of states, and avoid euphemisms for death. In AIDS cases, sometimes you face an ethical decision whether to state the cause of death. In this case, the deceased was an advocate for the disease.

Brett Stephen Huff entered into rest Monday. Beloved son of Martha and Edward Huff [of your town], and beloved brother of John of Ames, IA.; James of Scarsdale, N.Y., and Joseph of Dallas, TX.; dearly beloved grandson of Mary Margaret Huff, and nephew of Linda May Love of Detroit, MI. He was born [in your town] in 1970 and graduated from [your town's high school]. He earned a bachelor's degree in art from the University of Missouri in Columbia, MO. He owned his own graphics design firm [in your city] and had designed many brochures for area firms. A Mass of Christian Burial will be celebrated at 10:30 A.M. [use the day of the week for tomorrow] at Our Savior Church, 2020 Marysville Ave. Burial will be in Greenlawn Cemetery, 30 Main Street, [your town]. Contributions may be made to the AIDS Research Fund, Fernwood Hospital, 373 Paloma Street, [your town].

You suspect the cause of death is related to AIDS, and you call the family for information. Huff's mother confirms that he had AIDS. She says he died at her home [in your town]. She tells you that in the past year that he had spoken to school students in many area high schools to educate them about the disease. He was diagnosed with AIDS in 1994 when he was living in Los Angeles. He had worked for the Tucker Design Group in that city, but in 1995 he moved your city to be near his family, and he started his own firm, Huff Designs. "He wanted to alert people to ways of preventing AIDS," his mother says. "He tried to make people more sensitive to people who have the disease."

17-5. Feature Obituary

Write a feature obituary based on this information and any additional information you may gather. The day Jerry Garcia died, thousands of his fans flooded the Internet with messages of mourning and memories. You can gain additional information by using the Internet. You can find a home page for the Grateful Dead as well as several sites on the Web devoted to Garcia.

Here is some basic information from a variety of obituaries and articles about Garcia. Consider the ethical issue of whether you would include information about his drug use. When you include quotes by him or about him from previous interviews, attribute your source. Although the exact date of death is given here, use yesterday as your time frame.

Basic factual information:

Who: Jerome John Garcia, better known as "Jerry," the lead guitarist of the rock band, the Grateful Dead, died Aug. 9, 1995.

Age: 53

When: 4:23 a.m. (Pacific time – 7:23 a.m. EDT)

Where: In his bed at Serenity Knolls, a residential treatment center for drug addiction in Forest Knolls, Marin County, Calif.

Cause of death: Heart attack, according to the Marin County sheriff's office. Garcia had suffered from diabetes and general ill health for several years. He was an admitted user of heroin and psychedelic drugs such as LSD.

Survivors: Wife, Deborah Koons Garcia, a Marin County filmmaker, four daughters:
Heather, 32, Annabelle, 25, Teresa, 21 and Keelin, 6.

Funeral arrangements: Undecided at this time.

Background:

Born Jerome John Garcia in San Francisco on Aug. 1, 1942. Son of a band leader, Jose. Garcia was 5 when he witnessed the drowning death of his father. About that time Garcia lost the tip of his right middle finger in a wood-chopping accident. He was raised primarily by his mother, Ruth, who ran a saloon near the San Francisco waterfront. Became interested in playing electric guitar and painting when he was 15. Was a devoted reader of Beat Generation writer, Jack Kerouac. Quit high school after one year, worked as a salesman and a teacher for a while and joined the Army. After an early discharge, took classes at what is now the San Francisco Art Institute. Years later his abstract art was marketed in a line of neckties that earned him more than $30 million. Garcia even had an ice cream named after him, Ben & Jerry's Cherry Garcia ice cream.

Garcia formed the Warlocks rock group in 1964. This group became the Grateful Dead in 1966. Original members were Garcia, guitarist Bob Weir, Ron "Pigpen" McKernan, who died of a liver ailment in 1973, bass player Phil Lesh and drummer Bill Kreutzman. Drummer Mickey Hart

75

joined n 1967. It was a group that combined rock, bluegrass, blues and folk influences. Garcia was lead guitarist, composer and sometime vocalist. Among the band's best known songs were "Truckin'," "Casey Jones," and "Friend of the Devil." Its only top 10 hit was the 1987 song "Touch of Grey." The name "Warlocks" was already taken. In an interview with *Rolling Stone,* Garcia said, "We never decided to be the Grateful Dead. What happened was the Grateful Dead came up as a suggestion because we were at Phil's house one day; he had a big Oxford dictionary, I opened it up and the first thing I saw was The Grateful Dead. It said that on the page and it was so astonishing. It was truly weird, a truly weird moment." A grateful dead is a type of traditional British folk ballad in which a human helps a ghost of someone who has died recently find peace.

From *People* magazine: Garcia once reportedly said about psychedelic drugs: "I don't think there's anything else in life apart from a near-death experience that shows you how extensive the mind is."

In a 1993 interview with *The New Yorker,* he said he had given up drugs and taken up scuba diving. "It's an ecstatic experience," he said of scuba diving. "I love it almost as much as I love music."

From an interview with KFOG-FM in 1993: "Ideally I would just like to disappear gracefully and not leave behind any legacy to hang people up. I don't want people agonizing over who or what I was when I was here when I'm not here anymore. I would like to be thought of as a competent musician. That would be good. I'd like that."

In the past few years he had stopped smoking, cut down on drugs, and hired a personal fitness trainer.

The Grateful Dead was much more than a band. To millions of devoted fans, known as "Deadheads," it was a way of life. Many of these fans followed the group from concert to concert. The band was one of the most popular ever on the concert tour, grossing tens of millions of dollars each year from its concerts.

Speeches, News Conferences and Meetings

18

18-1. President's speech on death of Osama bin Laden

"It was nearly 10 years ago that a bright September day was darkened by the worst attack on the American people in our history. The images of 9/11 are seared into our national memory -- hijacked planes cutting through a cloudless September sky; the Twin Towers collapsing to the ground; black smoke billowing up from the Pentagon; the wreckage of Flight 93 in Shanksville, Pennsylvania, where the actions of heroic citizens saved even more heartbreak and destruction."

That is part of the speech President Barack Obama made about the killing of alQaida terrorist Osama bin Laden, the mastermind of the 9/11 attacks, on May 2, 2011.

Write a news story based on the speech, which you can read in text or hear it in audio or watch it in video form. Access it on the White House site at *http://www.whitehouse.gov/the-press-office/2011/05/02/remarks-president-osama-bin-laden.*

18-2: Graduation Speech

The speech was brilliant, funny and false. Supposedly Kurt Vonnegut had given this graduation speech at MIT in which he urged students to wear sunscreen, floss, dance and do one thing every day that scares you. But it was so clever that the speech was passed around the world via e-mail. Mary Schmich even got a copy of it, and that surprised her. This columnist for the *Chicago Tribune* contacted Vonnegut, who said he was also surprised to learn he had given the speech. He hadn't. It was a column Mary Schmich had written for the *Tribune*.

You can access the speech and the column through the Web site for this book or at *http://www.wesselenyi.com/speech.htm* or *http://www.ldb.org/vonnegut.htm.* If those links are no longer active, do a search for the Kurt Vonnegut graduation speech. It is posted in several sites.

18-3: News Conferences

Write a story based on a news conference in the briefing room of the White House. Select a briefing about a current issue in the news. You can read the text of the conferences or watch them in video form. Access White House news conferences at *http://www.whitehouse.gov/briefing-room/press-briefings.*

18-4. Meeting advance

The story you write before the meeting about issues the governmental body will discuss is often more important than the actual meeting story. The meeting advance informs readers so they have a chance to express their views at the meeting. You should get a copy of the meeting agenda a few days before the meeting. Write a meeting advance based on the following information:

You have received an agenda of the city commission meeting in your community. (Substitute commission for council or whatever your local city government body is called.) Read the following agenda and decide what item or items you think are worthy of an advance story. Here are some of the items on the agenda:

A. Consent agenda: All matters listed on the consent agenda are considered under one motion and will be enacted by one motion. There will be no separate discussion of those items. If discussion is desired, that item will be removed from the consent agenda and considered separately.

1. Review and approve minutes of various boards and commissions: City Commission meeting of previous week. Aviation Advisory Board meeting of previous week.

2. Approve renewal of the following licenses:
    a. Drinking establishments: Barb Wire's Steak House & Saloon, 2412 Iowa; Don's Steak House, 2176 East 23rd.

3. Bid item:
    a. Set bid date of Jan. 5 for annual lubricants contract (Public Works)

4. Approve on second and final reading, the following ordinances
    a. Ordinance No. 6354 annexing a 28.5 acre tract of land generally located south of Sixth Street and west of Wakarusa Drive.

5. Ordinance No. 6395 authorizing the issuance of $6,000,000 multi-family housing development revenue refunding bonds for Brandon Woods nursing home, 15th and Inverness Drive. (Approved by the commission on [date specified].

B. Consider the following regular agenda items:
1. Conduct a public hearing and consider adopting Resolution No. 5501 declaring house at 1222 Summit St. blighted.
    Action: Adopt Resolution No. 5501 if appropriate.
2. Consider proposed request for proposals for architectural consultant services related to proposed renovation and expansion of city art center.
    Action: Authorize request for proposals.

3. Receive feasibility update report from consulting team about building a public golf course.

> **Action: Receive and discuss study**

4. Receive staff report and draft ordinance prohibiting nudity in establishments selling intoxicating liquors.

> **Action: Receive staff report, direct placement of ordinance on next agenda.**

5. Consider approval of contract with Hamm Quarry Inc. for landfill services.

6. Consider appointments to various boards.

You have reviewed the agenda and have decided to focus on the proposed ordinance banning nudity or the consultants' report on the proposed city golf course. You call some of the commissioners (there are five) and find out they are really concerned about nudity in the local bars. City Manager Mike Wildgen tells you the concern was fostered because they received a proposal from a man who wants to start a bar featuring topless female dancers. The manager and commissioners don't tell you who he is, but they say they want to create an ordinance preventing nudity in bars or other establishments that serve liquor just to prevent someone from setting up such a place. Currently no bars in your city feature nude dancers.

Background:

The proposed ordinance would affect only businesses licensed to sell alcohol. It would not affect other "adult entertainment" establishments such as X-rated movie theaters. The proposed ordinance says: "Alcohol-licensed establishments that offer nude dancing foster and promote incidents of criminal activity, can and do adversely affect property values, can and do contribute to neighborhood decay and blight, and do create direct exposures to health risks and potential health hazards."

Johnson County, a neighboring county, is being sued by a club and several nude dancers who say that the county's ban on nude dancing is unconstitutional.

Here are some of the commissioners' comments:

Commissioner Bob Walters: "I'm not a prude. But I don't think that nude entertainment in any form should be allowed in any business with access to the public. Sometimes I don't understand why we can't do what we think is in the best interests of the community."

Commissioner Bob Schumm: "We just don't need it (nudity). We're doing fine without it. This is a wholesome city, a good place to raise a family and we don't need all the problems that go along with (adult entertainment)."

Commissioner Shirley Martin-Smith: "I am not into banning free speech or banning anything, but I am into putting some controls on entertainment that is not a benefit to the community. People are just amazed that this even needs to be an issue. I think the point of the ordinance is to eliminate the possibility of nudity as entertainment in the city. I think we just have to pursue it and see where it takes us, which is what we do on a lot of issues."

County Chief Deputy Counselor, LeeAnne Gillaspie: The legal basis for restricting behavior in such clubs was firmly stated in the 21st Amendment to the Constitution, which outlawed Prohibition and gave states the power to restrict alcohol consumption. She said once the law moves away from alcohol (such as regulating juice bars, for example), the issue moves into the First Amendment and freedom of expression guarantees.

The meeting will be conducted at 6:30 p.m. Monday in your city hall (give the address) or use Sixth and Massachusetts streets.

Based on a story from the *Lawrence* (Kan.) *Daily Journal-World.* Used with permission.

18-5. School board meeting

Read the following script of a school board meeting and write a story, choosing the most interesting item for your focus.

The Rockville School Board is conducting its weekly meeting at 7 p.m. in the school administration building, at 2500 Addison Place. (You may substitute the name of the school board in your town for this exercise.) Write a story based on the scenario that follows.

School board members are as follows: Alfred C. Robertson (president), William Harold, Maria Santana, Peter Bodine (Board secretary), Denise Davis. The meeting begins with a motion to approve the minutes of the last meeting, and the board unanimously approves.

Robertson: Next item on the agenda is to receive bids for three new school buses.

Bodine: We've got kind of a deal here. One bus company, Sierra Busing, has entered a bid of $23,520. Now that's for a normal bus that can hold 84 students. Another company, Buses Unlimited, offers an 84-seater that runs on diesel for $24,000 even. The Springfield Valley Unified School District has offered one of their used buses for $12,000. Again it holds 84 people, but it's got 80,000 miles on it and is a '78 model.

Davis: Is 80,000 too many?

Bodine: No, I don't think so. I'd recommend that bus.

Santana: Why are they selling it?

Bodine: The district is growing smaller and they don't need it. And they're in a budget crunch.

Davis: But why this particular one? Something wrong with it?

Bodine: No. Our district's mechanic checked it out and said it's fine. Purrs like a kitten were his exact, if unoriginal, words.

Davis: I move we accept the bid of $12,000 from the Springfield Valley Unified School District for the offered bus.

Robertson: Do I hear a second.

Harold: Second.

Robertson: All in favor say aye. (Board unanimously approves.)

Robertson: Next item on the agenda is the appropriation of funds to put the basketball team up in a hotel for three days. The high school's team won the division tournament and is going to the state finals in Phoenix. If they continue their winning ways, they will have to stay up there at least three days. The appropriation requests $125 per night so the basketball team can compete in state playoffs for as long as they need to stay in Phoenix.

(The motion is seconded, and the board unanimously approves.)

Robertson: The next request is from the high school librarian for money. Mr. Secretary, will you please read the request?

Bodine: I have a request here from Mrs. Phyllis Laird, head librarian. It reads: "In order to keep our library in tune with modern times, update reference materials, replace damaged and lost books, and add new magazines to our subscription list, we are asking for $543 before the next school year. A well-stocked library is a necessary part of a student's education, and so I hope you will grant our request." Mrs. Laird goes on to list how the money would be spent.

Robertson: For a set of new encyclopedias to replace our 1975 versions, a new set of science-oriented encyclopedias, magazine subscriptions to *Time, Newsweek, Sports Illustrated, Boys Life* and something called *Dragon*. I don't know what that is for sure. Then she's got an almanac and other reference materials and about 200 books. You all have read the lists, right?

All: Nod and mumble in the affirmative.

Robertson: What do you think of Mrs. Laird's choices?

Harold: I have no problems with the request, and I move we vote to authorize the appropriation for $543 for the school library.

Robertson: Well, before we take a second on your motion, I think we ought to discuss these books and magazines a little.

Harold: What's to discuss? They're all fine books.

Bodine: I'm not so sure I want to agree to this authorization. Some of these books, I think, are questionable. I have no objections to Shakespeare or even books like *Megatrends* or Lee Iacocca's autobiography. But some of these bother me. As an example I give this one – Kurt Vonnegut's book, *Slaughterhouse Five*. There are some sections in here that deal with sex, others put down the United States. It's strange fare and I'm not so sure Rockville kids need to read stuff like that.

Robertson: Well, I had some reservations on some of these myself, Mr. Bodine. I've heard that this *Catcher in the Rye* by J.D. Salinger, down near the bottom of the list, is about homosexuality. I don't think our students ought to be educated about such topics.

Harold: Mr. President, am I to assume you don't want to approve the request for money because of some of the books on the list?

Robertson: No, Mr. Harold. I'm willing to approve the request, just minus some of the books and magazines.

Harold: That sounds like censorship to me.

Bodine: I think it's censorship, Bill, but it's good censorship. We're concerned for these children, and I think that some of these books can only hinder a student's development. We should be careful here. Would you want students to read a book that perpetuates racial stereotypes? Have you ever read *Huckleberry Finn?* That novel just reeks with the degradation of blacks.

Robertson: I don't even think we need to look at some of them. Students don't need to read trash. Though, I wonder what you've got against Huck Finn. I read it as a boy, and I think it's a fine novel.

Santana: I think I agree with Mr. Bodine. I try to watch my kids. I've read reports in newspapers about kids who read comic books or those sword and sorcery books and then go out and play Dungeons and Dragons and then end up committing suicide. Maybe we should look at these things.

Harold: Maria, do you monitor what your kids watch on TV?

Santana: No, not really.

Harold: So you let your kids watch something where people run around shooting 1,000 rounds of ammunition per show. Now, do your kids run out and grab machine guns and start shooting each other? No, so why would books have that effect?

Bodine: I think it's the potential for that effect. A student who is violent or depressed may be pushed over the edge.

Harold: You can't protect them from everything. And in the meantime, they could lose something valuable. It's important that a child reads, and I don't care if the kid reads cigarette packages or *War and Peace.* The important thing is that they are learning how words work and how to communicate.

Bodine: OK, then, why don't we put *Playboy* in the library? So long as reading is the only thing that's important.

Harold: Get serious, Peter. You know I'm not advocating that.

Bodine: So you will censor, just to a different degree.

Davis: I've been sitting here watching you debate. Twenty-five years ago we had this same type of discussion. But back then we were talking about John Steinbeck. A number of parents were concerned that the subject matter in *The Grapes of Wrath* would be too shocking to students. They believed it portrayed a world and an attitude of negativism and pessimism. A book is neither good nor bad. It all depends on how it is used and read. I would give students the option. Open our library to different books and let them decide. I don't believe it is our place to dictate what a student can and cannot read.

Santana: Well, are we going to vote on something? Should have a new motion.

Bodine: I move we set a public hearing two weeks from today to get parents' reactions to these books.

Santana: I second the motion.

Harold: Mr. President, I wonder exactly what that will accomplish. We have over 200 books on this list. I doubt that the public has read all of them. I doubt we've read all of them. You're still talking as if you intend to censor if parents say it's all right with them. Are we each going to vote on 200 books? Where do you start and stop?

Davis: I agree with Bill. Even if we decide that the board has the power to censor, I believe it would be too difficult to decide what should be censored. And that is the strongest argument for not censoring. The world is out there, good and bad. We can't stop it from touching the children. Teach them what's good and bad and use those books as examples. But don't close their minds.

Robertson: We have a motion on the floor to schedule a public hearing regarding the book list Mrs. Laird has submitted. I'd like a roll call vote. How do you vote?

Davis: No.

Harold: No.

Santana: Yes.

Bodine: Yes.

Robertson: Aye. The ayes have it. By a vote of 3-2 a public hearing will be scheduled for Friday, April 18, at 7 p.m. here to discuss the book list and appropriation request.

Member of the audience: You're all nuts. I'll be back here in two weeks to tell you that. I can't believe you're so damn foolish.

Harold: (addressing the audience member) I believe they're that foolish. I'll vote against every stupid goddam thing you propose.

Robertson: Do we have a motion to close this meeting?

Santana: So moved.

The board seconded and approved the motion, and the meeting was adjourned.

This script was adapted from one written by journalism students at the University of Arizona.

Government and Statistical Stories

19

19-1. Statistics – crime rates

Assume that these are the annual crime rate statistics for your state, released by your state Bureau of Investigation. Decide which findings are the most dramatic to report. Using the statistics and information from sources, write a news story. Do not flood your lead with statistics. Analyze the most interesting information and write a summary lead based on that. You don't need all the statistics in your story, but you should include the most important ones. Your story will be accompanied by a graphic.

Type	Last year	This year	Percent change
Murder	138	204	47.8
Forcible rape	1,518	1,584	4.3
Robbery	2,982	3,637	22
Aggravated assault	12,673	13,429	6
Burglary	39,626	38,869	-1.9
Larceny/theft	127,336	131,305	3.1
Motor vehicle theft	14,094	14,346	1.8
Total	198,367	203,364	2.5

Other statistics from your State Bureau of Investigation:

Based on statistics for the current year, bureau officials say that in your state:

* Someone becomes a victim of violent crime every 30 minutes.

* An assault is committed (in your state) every 41 minutes.

* A rape is committed every 5 hours and 46 minutes.

* A murder is committed every 63 hours.

Comments from sources:

From Mike Stiers, division chief of the bureau: "The increase in violence is what really concerns us. They're either bashing them in the head or shooting them when it's not necessary. The increase in violent crime reflects a greater social problem that can't be solved by police alone. We're losing the battle here. People need to realize this. They need to demand of their legislators, both state and municipal, that they don't want to live like this."

From Julie Reaman, a therapist with Ending the Violence Effectively, a counseling group for victims: Increased publicity about sexual assault and incest may have boosted the reporting rate.

From Anne Byrne of the Rape Awareness and Assistance Program: "I don't think it's a huge increase in the amount of reports. I think more sexual assaults are going on. I don't know why; it's alarming."

From Bob Allen, county undersheriff: "I think it has to do with a general downward trend in morality, a breakdown in family. That's a community function, everybody pulling together and starting to work together. Many murders are committed by family or acquaintances. I personally feel that people who do it are people who know each other. That's typical of homicide. You always hurt the one you love."

Based on a story from the *Rocky Mountain News*. Used with permission.

19-2. Weather statistics

Was it the hottest or coldest season, the wettest or driest? People like to read about weather. So reporters periodically have to write weather stories summarizing the statistics for the month, the season or the year. Here are some annual statistics – minus December – for three counties in South Florida, where weather is important news. Compare the statistics and find an angle for your story.

The following statistics compare rainfall levels (in inches) for the months with normal rainfall. Months are divided into the normally wet and dry seasons for Broward, Palm Beach, and Dade counties. You are writing this story in November as a weather roundup for that month for a newspaper that serves these three counties. Assume you are writing this for the current year. This chart will run with your story. The only comment you have is from Geoff Shaughnessy, meteorologist for the South Florida Water Management District, who said the rain in November came from moisture-laden weather fronts that stalled over South Florida, a phenomenon that is more typical for October. Write a very brief story, approximately six to eight inches, or about a page and a half of double-spaced typed copy. Assume that you have a weather forecast of a new front coming through that is expected to bring more rain.

Dry	Broward	Palm Beach	Dade	Norm
Jan.	2.88	1.89	2.15	2.41
Feb.	2.49	3.86	1.64	2.19
March	1.97	2	3.01	2.7
April	3.63	3.05	2.75	3.43
Wet				
May	0.94	1.1	0.81	5.87
June	16.84	16.45	20.95	8.1
July	3.35	2.91	3.5	6.41
Aug.	8.4	8.38	11.41	6.83
Sept.	3.81	6.81	4.07	8.52

Oct.	1.88	1.27	1.63	7.84
(continued)				
Dry				
Nov.	6.91	11.14	6.41	2.84
Dec.	——	——	——	2.02
Total	53.09	58.86	58.33	59.16

19-3. City budget story

Your city commission (or whatever your local governing body is called) is considering a proposed budget for the coming year. The budget was presented to the commission yesterday by the city manager. Read the following budget information and analyze where expenditures increased or decreased the most. Decide what kinds of questions you might ask the city manager. Look at the tax rate (the mill levy) and decide if it has increased, decreased or stayed the same. Then, using the chart on how to figure your taxes, explain in your story what that rate will mean for the owner of a home assessed at $15,000, an average assessment in your community. The city assesses homes at 15 percent of market value, so a home worth $100,000 would be assessed at $15,000 for tax purposes. Use an impact lead telling readers what this budget means to them and explaining how their money will be spent. Comments from the manager follow.

General operating budget – summary of expenditures

Item	Last year	Current Year	Proposed next year
Public works	573,089	784,700	864,000
Water/sewage	9,117,586	10,360	10,977,027
Parks/recreation	634,945	697,400	810,800
Business improvement	0	0	83,689
Employee benefits	3,102,708	3,446,800	3,380,450
Bonds/interest	3,643,654	3,125,413	4,252,000
Sanitation	2,241,201	2,641,200	2,949,540
Police	2,881,738	3,101,800	3,197,350
Fire	2,014,616	2,191,750	23,433,050
Animal control	581,390	128,550	130,120
Library	581,390	662,180	723,913
General operations	6,554,490	7,227,339	6,927,180
Total	**31,478,139**	**34,366,890**	**36,639,119**
Mills	**42.2**	**42**	**42.2**

(Continued on next page)

Revenues: About 57% of revenues come from property taxes. Other sources include $15,805,749 from various taxes such as:

Property tax	$ 20,833,370
Gas taxes	$ 1,089,440
Alcohol	$ 230,133
Guest tax	$ 185,000
Water/sewer	$ 10,977,027
Sanitation	$ 2,949,540
Fed. revenue sharing	$ 25,000
Parking meters	$ 265,920
Business improvements	$ 83,689
Total	**$ 36,639,119**

Where the money goes

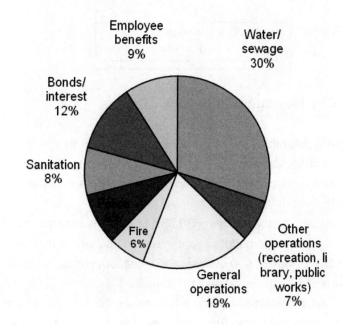

Employee benefits 9%

Water/sewage 30%

Bonds/interest 12%

Sanitation 8%

Fire 6%

General operations 19%

Other operations (recreation, library, public works) 7%

How to figure your property tax

1. Write the assessed value of your property in Box A. This is the amount your property is appraised for   tax purposes, not the amount of money it would sell for on the market.   For example, if you have a   house worth $100,000 and the city assesses it at 15% of its value for taxes, your assessed value is $15,000.

2. Divide the figure in Box A by 1,000 because a mill is $1 tax on every $1,000 of assessed value. Write the result in Box B.

3. Write the mill levy in Box C. For this city, the levy proposed is 42.2 mills.

4. Multiply the figures in Boxes B and C. Write the result in Box D. This is the amount of taxes you will owe to the city.

```
┌─Calculate your tax rate ──────────┐
│                                    │
│  ┌──────────────────────────────┐  │
│  │ Assessed value:    A         │  │
│  └──────────────────────────────┘  │
│  ┌──────────────────────────────┐  │
│  │ Divided by 1,000:  B         │  │
│  └──────────────────────────────┘  │
│  ┌──────────────────────────────┐  │
│  │ Mill levy:              C    │  │
│  └──────────────────────────────┘  │
│                                    │
│  ┌──────────────────────────────┐  │
│  │ Multiply B X C =Taxes:       │  │
│  │                    D         │  │
│  └──────────────────────────────┘  │
└────────────────────────────────────┘
```

Remarks by City Manager Michael A. Thrifty

I am hereby submitting the recommended budget for the coming fiscal year commencing in July. The current fiscal budget is presented as a working document for your consideration. (City commissioners must conduct public hearings before they can adopt it. Public hearings will be scheduled at the end of the month.)

The proposed budget totals $36,639,119 as compared to the current budget of $34,366,890.   The proposed budget is presented to you with a minimal increase in the tax rate of 42.20 mills or $42.20 per $1,000 of assessed valuation, compared to 42.10 mills for the current year.   We have estimated the assessed valuation at the time of budget preparation to be $493,681,760.   The real estate valuation has grown $5,100,000 in the past year, which will provide us with more revenue from property taxes without raising taxes.   The budget concentrates on providing current staff levels. However, the growth we are experiencing places pressure on current staffing levels in public safety, public works and parks maintenance.

Our bond indebtedness continues to increase. Part of that is due to a $1 million bond issue voters approved in the last election to fund a new recreation center.

Providing water and sewage treatment for our growing population continues to be a significant portion of our budget.

Specific recommendations in this budget are as follows:

- A 3% salary increase for all employees

- The amount of refuse collected, number of customers added and size of area serviced for the Sanitation Department has significantly increased in the past five years. I am recommending addition of one residential crew supervisor, one commercial crew supervisor, two commercial drivers, and two commercial loaders. Two years ago city crews collected 34,018 tons of refuse; last year it was 41,357 tons and to date the rate will result in 44,734 tons.
- Two of the downtown parking lots will be overlaid with asphalt this summer, and I am recommending $25,000 be allocated in the parking meter fund to continue the maintenance program.
- The Business Improvement District is included for the first time. The income from this district with a 1 percent tax for improvement of the downtown business area will be the revenue source.

Respectfully submitted,
City Manager Michael A. Thrifty

(In addition to city taxes, residents pay county and school taxes, but those taxes are levied in separate budgets by the school district and the county. The total tax rate last year for city, county and school taxes was 127 mills.)

19-4. Caffeine consumption

How much caffeine are you consuming? If you are drinking herbal tea to cut down on your coffee consumption, you might be getting almost as much caffeine in your ginseng tea. If you eat Ben & Jerry's coffee yogurt ice cream, you could get almost as much caffeine as by drinking coffee. Is caffeine dangerous? Write a story about caffeine by using statistics and press releases from the Center for Science in the Public Interest. You can supplement your statistics with interviews of your classmates and friends about their favorite drinks, drugs (Excedrin and the like) and candy. If the caffeine statistics are no longer available, check the Web site for other reports containing statistics. You can access the CPSI caffeine chart on the center's site at: *http://www.cspinet.org/new/cafchart.htm.*

Crime and Punishment 20

20-1. Crime statistics

Access Security on Campus, a website of college and university crime statistics and write a story comparing crime rates for your school (if they are available) with those of other schools near you or of your choice. Check out other links as well. Interview a law enforcement officer in your university about problems on campus. If your community or campus police department has a website, check it against the national site. You can access Security on Campus through the website for this book or directly at *http://www.securityoncampus.org*.

20-2. Mummy saga – a continuing crime story

This exercise, which will give you practice writing a continuing police/court case, is based on a real story, but the names have been changed. Write each part based on the information you have. Do not read ahead because you may not use anything in future exercises. However, when you write the next day's episode, you should always recap the basics of what happened. If your instructor prefers, you may change the locations to your own county.

People and places involved:

Location: rural Knoxville, about 10 miles east of Galesburg in Knox County, Ill.

Knox County Sheriff Mark Shoemaker (source of most information)

Carol Truelove, 48, wife of the deceased. She is a registered nurse.

Carl Truelove, last seen alive in May, eight years ago, at age 40. His body was found in mummified condition.

Richard G. Cuspid, 56, a former Chicago-area dentist. He was a houseguest of Mrs. Truelove for the past year.

Curt Cousins, 44, of Cudahy, Wisconsin. He is Carol Truelove's cousin. He helped authorities gain entrance to her home.

Roger Cutter, Knox County coroner

Craig Truelove, 14, son of Carol Truelove

Cindy Truelove, 17, daughter of Carol Truelove

Roger Truelove, a Chicago attorney and brother of the late Carl Truelove. He fought to keep authorities from the house. He died five years ago of cancer.

Judge Ronald Tenold, presiding judge in Knox County District Court

1. Day One

Write a brief story based on this information, all of which comes from Knox County Sheriff Mark Shoemaker. You are writing on deadline for an afternoon paper or early evening newscast and cannot check much out, so this is a brief report. Use today as your time frame. The broadcast story should run :30 as an anchor reader.

Shoemaker conducts a press conference at noon and says that sheriff's deputies have arrested Carol Truelove on a charge of failing to report a death. It is a Class A misdemeanor, punishable by a fine up to $1,000 and up to 364 days in jail. Shoemaker says his deputies entered Truelove's house at 11:30 a.m. today and found a corpse in a mummified state. The corpse, believed to be Carl Truelove, was wrapped in blankets and was lying on a bed in a back room of the house. Carl Truelove had not been seen for eight years. Carol Truelove had told people he was very ill, and she would not let anyone see him.

Police had no probable cause to search the house previously. They entered today, despite her objections, because a relative had let them in the house and told them about the corpse. Shoemaker will not release the relative's name. Shoemaker says of the corpse: "His skin was dried up like shoe leather, and he just shriveled up. We believe he was kept a long time in a basement lounge chair. Although it was obvious he had been dead for eight years, the family sincerely thought he was fine, the way he was being treated. They changed his clothes and bedding just like he was sick. There's also evidence that they moved him around the house to different rooms and chairs. There was no strong odor in the home and something had to be done at the time of death to preserve the body."

He said the body had on pajama bottoms, underwear and socks. "Everything was very neat, very clean." He would not speculate what was done. An autopsy is expected at the end of this week. Foul play is not suspected, but the incident is under investigation. Mrs. Truelove's houseguest, Richard G. Cuspid, also was arrested on the same misdemeanor charge. They will be arraigned tomorrow morning. You have many questions, but Shoemaker says he will not comment further until the couple has been officially charged and arraigned. Both suspects were booked and held in the county jail.

2. Day Two

The arraignment. Use today as your time frame. The news is very brief, but don't forget to include your background for both print and broadcast.
The broadcast version should be a :20 anchor reader.

Judge Ronald Tenold presided in Knox County Circuit Court at 9 a.m. today. Carol Truelove and Richard Cuspid both pleaded guilty to the misdemeanor charge of failing to report a death. The judge did not sentence them at this time. He ordered a pre-sentence investigation. The two were released on their own recognizance. Carol Truelove did not speak other than to plead guilty. Cuspid complained that he had not been allowed to post his $100 bail because the sheriff's office would not accept silver coins as payment. He also complained of conditions at the jail and said he had not had anything to eat or drink because "I only eat pure food" and his requests for distilled water, tuna and halibut had been denied. Write your story on deadline.

91

Sheriff Shoemaker tells you after the arraignment that the charge was the only one he could make because "eight years is not exactly timely reporting of a death." The coroner is still checking cause of death. State law requires people to notify the coroner of a death within 24 hours.

3. Day Two - next step

You have just written your deadline story when you get a call from Sheriff Mark Shoemaker's office. He is going to have a press conference in 30 minutes. At the press conference, he gives you this information; rewrite your story for print and broadcast.

We have rearrested Carol Truelove and Richard Cuspid on additional charges. They were arrested within minutes of their release as they were leaving the courthouse and were taken back to jail pending another arraignment later today on the new charges. Mrs. Truelove has been charged with one count of forgery for allegedly signing her husband's name to fabricate a power of attorney eight years ago. Cuspid was charged with one count of conspiracy to commit forgery for signing his name to the document as a witness. Both are forgery charges, punishable by up to three years in prison. The document gave Carol the right to control money in Carl's bank account. You have many questions about the case and the sheriff gives you this information in response:

"Apparently Carol Truelove and members of her family believed the corpse of Carl Truelove was still alive. They felt he could talk with them and everyone in the family admits to communicating with them. It's just very bizarre. We are currently investigating religious aspects of this."

He says Carol Truelove wants her husband's body returned to her home, but the sheriff's office is checking on health codes to see if this can be prevented legally. He says he and his deputies had checked on Carl Truelove over the years but had never been able to gain admittance to the house. He says Carl, a bookkeeper for Drainclean Plumbing, failed to report to work and the owner had notified the sheriff's office. But he says he had no probable cause to get a search warrant, so he just took Carol's word for it that her husband was very ill and could not have visitors. He says Cuspid had been her houseguest for a year and is believed to be part of a religious group or cult that believes in some sort of healing involving dentistry and herbs and special diet. He says Cuspid was introduced by Carol Truelove's late brother-in-law, Roger Truelove, who drew up the power-of-attorney document. Carl Truelove was a diabetic. The coroner is still checking cause of death. He says he gained access to the house when Carol Truelove's cousin, Curt Cousins, had visited the house and then notified the sheriff's office of the corpse. Cousins let the sheriff's deputies in the house. The children, who are honor students in school, have been temporarily placed in foster care. He stills says no foul play is suspected in connection with the corpse. Write your story for a later edition of today's paper or the evening newscast.

(continued)

4. Day Three

Carol Truelove and Richard Cuspid were arraigned yesterday on the new charges before Judge Ronald Tenold. Both pleaded not guilty. Tenold set bail at $20,000 for each, but neither could post it, so they remain in the county jail. In related developments, the coroner, Roger Cutter, ruled that Carl Truelove, a lifelong diabetic, died about eight years ago from insulin shock (caused by a lack of insulin). Cutter said the mummified body was dehydrated but had been preserved by some herbal mixture. The children remain in protective custody. The sheriff said the state is still trying to get an order to bury the remains of the corpse. The print and broadcast stories are briefs. The broadcast version is a 20 anchor reader.

Epilogue: Not for your story. The woman was convicted of forgery and received two years probation and her houseguest was also convicted and sentenced to 30 months on probation. The corpse was finally buried by a state order, because officials feared the wife would take it back into her home and continue tending to it.

20-3. Hourglass crime story

Write this story in hourglass form. Be careful to attribute any accusatory statements to the police. You may try a creative lead because there were no fatalities or injuries.

You call the local sheriff's department. A spokesman for the Pasco Sheriff's Department [or your county's department], Jon Powers, tells you that five boys, one 11, one 14 and three age 15, were arrested yesterday. He says he cannot release their names because they are juveniles. He said the boys have all been charged with burglary to a vehicle. He says they all admitted to the crime.

You ask for details and he tells you that they were charged with breaking into a food supply truck with a crowbar and stealing assorted boxes of candy, cookies and snacks. He says the goods were worth more than $500. Powers gives you this scenario: The stealing started late last night when two of the boys, who are brothers, saw the truck in the parking lot. The older brother, 15, took a crowbar from a neighbor's yard and pried the padlock off the truck's rear door. He and his brother, 11, then took a carton of candy from the truck. They later told the other boys what they had done.

Powers says the boys tried to carry the goodies home, but the boxes became too heavy for them. They left a 50-pound box of Milky Ways on a bench in front of a Winn Dixie supermarket (according to the police report). You ask what other kinds of candy and snacks they took. Powers says the stolen material included the case of Milky Way bars, boxes of cheese crackers and popcorn and a carton of chocolate creme-filled cookies. You ask what kind of truck it was. He says the truck was Lance Inc. food truck that was in a parking lot on Darlington Road. Lance supplies food for vending machines.

Based on a story from the *St. Petersburg* (Fla.) *Times.* Used with permission.

20-4. Court case

Write a story based on a court opinion for a case in your state (or other if you prefer). Access Findlaw from the Web site for this book or directly at: *http://www.findlaw.com*

Click into Cases and Codes and then click on State Cases and Codes until you find your state. Check any of the court cases; the Court of Appeals cases are often interesting. Find a case and write a news story based on the court document. For example, here is an Alaska case about a man who attacked his ex-wife because he couldn't find his wallet. It is rich in detail. *http://www.touchngo.com/ap/html/ap-1607.htm*

Disasters, Weather and Tragedies

21

21-1. Airplane crash – Day One – Breaking news story (for print, online, mobile or social media and the Web)

Access this information and print a copy of these notes for this assignment. This is a deadline writing assignment. Limit yourself to about one hour writing time if possible—no more than 90 minutes for the complete story. Write a brief breaking-news story for the Web as soon as you have enough information. If you want to localize the story, substitute local sources, your nearest metropolitan airport and local hospitals for those named in the story. You may find conflicting information, as you would at the scene of any major disaster. You will have to decide how to handle it. Here is the information:

It is 3 p.m. You hear on the police radio that ambulances are racing to the Kansas City (Mo.) International Airport and that the Kansas City Fire Department is also responding to a call for help. A plane has crashed. You call the city police department and find out that a major commercial airliner has crashed, but you can't get anything more at this time.

You call the airport public information department and learn that the plane was a Delta Airlines jetliner from Dallas-Fort Worth International Airport that was due to land in Missouri at 2:30 p.m. The spokeswoman, P.R. Informer, tells you the plane crashed at 2:55 p.m. and is in flames, but she can tell you nothing more at this time.

You may write a breaking-news alert for your website, Twitter or mobile media at this time.

Your editor sends you to the airport to get the main story and another reporter to get quotes from people at the terminal for a color sidebar. A third reporter is on standby in the city room waiting to hear from you to determine the extent of the crash and to make phone calls to get additional information for your story. This reporter will get background from clips and call hospitals.

It is raining hard. Lightning slices through the sky frequently as you drive to the airport. You arrive at the airport and head for the Delta Airlines terminal in the C concourse. You race to the runway where the plane has crashed and see the charred pieces of metal strewn over the edge of the runway. The tail section is intact; it has broken away from the rest of the plane and is resting on a stretch of grass, about 150 feet from the edge of the runway. The area is already cordoned off. The scene is chaotic. Scores of airport fire trucks and fire apparatus from all fire

95

companies in the city and county, as well as ambulances, are at the scene. Firefighters are still spraying foam on the smoldering wreckage. The entire area is a sea of foam, as though the runway had been blanketed by a heavy snowstorm. Rescue workers are carrying bodies on stretchers. People are screaming.

It appears as though the nose of the plane exploded on contact with the ground, just at the edge of the runway. Wreckage is strewn over about 500 square feet. Body parts, suitcases, pieces of clothing and mangled shreds of metal litter the ground.

You get to a roped-off area and talk to a man who seems to be in charge. He is the airport fire marshal, John L. Smoke. He has no specific figures, but he says it appears that more than 100 people are dead. The plane exploded as it hit the edge of the runway on its approach for a landing, he says. He says it seems that about 25 people who were in the rear of the plane survived, but he has no official count.

Smoke says the airport authorities are taking care of the survivors who were not injured, but he is not specific about where they were taken. As he talks to you, injured passengers on stretchers moan and wail as they are loaded into ambulances. You are not allowed to get near them. Bodies draped in yellow plastic are still at the site. You count at least 20, but there is so much confusion you can't get an accurate count or even a good estimate.

You have been on the scene about 30 minutes, and by now the flames are out, helped by pouring rain. The tail section is so covered with foam that you cannot make out any details. A dozen fire engines surround the plane.

You head back to the terminal to talk to airport authorities. On your way back, you corner an ambulance driver, Samuel L. Savior. He tells you this is the worst experience he has ever had. "It isn't the injuries that strike me," he says. "I have never seen so much terror in people's eyes. It's horrifying."

In the airport, you get to P.R. Informer, information director for the airport. She is conducting a news conference in a few minutes. At the news conference, she says it was a Delta Airlines L-1011, Flight 313 from Dallas International Airport. The plane was made by Lockheed Aircraft. She says many of the passengers originated at Kennedy International Airport in New York and changed planes in Dallas for the final destination to Kansas City. She says the three-engine plane was carrying 275 passengers and a crew of six flight attendants (plus the pilot and two co-pilots).

At this point you should write a brief version for the Web, which you will continually update.

It appears as though at least 200 people are dead, including the pilot and two co-pilots. Informer says there are 25 survivors, and she does not know the fate of others who are not accounted for yet. She says a passenger list will not be released to the press until all the families of the passengers have been contacted —which could take at least a full day and perhaps longer. Airport and Delta Airlines personnel will work around the clock, she says.

In answer to your questions, Informer says the dead are being held in an airport hangar until they can be identified. The injured are being taken to area hospitals. Most of them are being taken to the University of Kansas Medical Center, St. Luke's Hospital and Liberty Hospital.

"This is a terrible tragedy," Informer says. "We are doing everything we can to notify relatives as quickly as we can. This is the worst thing that has ever happened in this state. It was a freak accident. We flew 2 million passengers in and out of this airport last year and our safety record was perfect. The only thing we can ascertain at this time is that the weather may have been a factor."

"If the weather was so bad, why wasn't the airport closed?" you ask.

"We safely land and depart planes all the time in thunderstorms, and this one did not seem prohibitive to air traffic," Informer says. "We have just completed a $65 million airport expansion project, and our airport is one of the safest in the country." She tells you the airport is closed to all traffic at this time and will remain closed until all rescue operations are completed. You check later and find out that the airport reopened five hours later, but the northeast concourse will remain closed indefinitely. It will be at least three days and maybe a week before officials from the Federal Aviation Administration and the National Transportation Safety Board have investigated and the wreckage is removed.

About 50 firefighters and eight units responded.

A Delta Airlines spokesman, I.M. Devastated, says the plane had six flight attendants and three crew members. He says the pilot was Captain Ted Connors, the co-pilot was Rudy Price, and Nick Nassick was the flight engineer. All three crew members are confirmed dead. He says Connors was from Fort Worth and was 57. He had been with the airline for 30 years and was one of its most experienced pilots. He was due to retire in three years. Price was 42 and had been with the airline for 14 years. He was from Lithonia, Ga. Nassick was 43. He was from Atlanta. He had been with the airline for nine years. Devastated says it appears that the only survivors were in the rear of the plane. He says he does not know the fate of the flight attendants. He is not releasing their names until he is sure their relatives have been notified. "The airline is doing everything possible," he says.

Devastated says Delta Airlines has 35 L-1011s. He says this was a 125-ton jumbo jet with a capacity of 300 passengers and 11 crew members. "This is a terrible tragedy, and our company will do everything we can to give support to the loved ones of those who perished and those who were injured," he says.

Investigators from the National Transportation Safety Board arrive on the scene shortly before 6 p.m. They say they are looking for the black box that records the pilot's communications. Retired Coast Guard Adm. Patrick Bursely, a member of the NTSB team, says he has no official cause of the crash, but weather factors such as wind shears are suspected because of the violent thunderstorms that struck Kansas City shortly before the plane crashed.

Wind shears, which are sudden and violent changes in wind direction, were responsible for several other plane crashes, including the crash of a Pan American World Airways 727 jetliner that crashed after takeoff from Kenner, La., in 1982, killing 153 people.

You head for the Delta Airlines counter. Hundreds of people are jamming the area. Many are canceling flights. Others are waiting gloomily until the airport reopens. Some are sitting on their luggage; others are lounging on the carpet.

Others are in the airport bar. You see no sign of survivors or relatives. Airport personnel have taken them into a private room and will not allow the press to talk to them. At this point you meet up with Sarah Sidekick, the reporter who was assigned to get color. She says she was able to get some quotes from survivors and relatives before airline personnel got to them.

97

It is now 6:30 p.m. You call the city desk, and the editor tells you to come back and start writing for the next day's print edition (or for the 11 p.m. broadcast news edition). You are the main writer on the story. (In reality, someone inside the newsroom probably would be assigned to be the main writer, and you would stay at the scene.) You will take some of the color quotes from Sarah Sidekick and notes from other reporters who have done hospital checks, background and telephone interviews with officials.

Sidekick is writing a color sidebar with more reactions, but you need some quotes from her for your story.

Here is the information gathered by the other reporters:

Weather report: Severe thunderstorms started in the Kansas City area about 2 p.m. Winds in some parts of the city were as high as 65 mph. Trees were knocked down, and severe flooding occurred in some areas. The storm lasted for about two hours and then blew toward the east.

From survivor Milton I. Goldberg, 65, of New York: He was on his way to visit his daughter, Millie Muffin, 35, of 3600 Westbrooke, Lawrence (a city 30 miles west of Kansas City). "It was terrifying. Everyone was screaming and shouting. They were diving out of their seats and pushing. Some were getting trampled on. One of the flight attendants grabbed me and threw me out the emergency door. I'm lucky to be alive. I heard this earsplitting crackle. I think it was lightning. I was sitting in the back of the plane. I looked out the window and saw the wing crack. The next thing I heard was a deafening explosion. From that point on, all I heard was screaming. The cabin began to fill with smoke. There was mass panic." He began to sob and couldn't continue.

From Martha Mayhem, 59, of 2300 Harvard Road, Lawrence: She was waiting at the Delta Airlines gate where the passengers were supposed to come in when she heard the news of the crash. "I was waiting for my fiancé. He was my childhood sweetheart. I waited for him all these years. I never married, but he did. Then we met in New York a year ago. He was widowed. We fell in love all over again. We were planning to get married this week. I can't believe that he isn't walking through that door. He told me he would take the first seat on the plane so he could get off fastest and never keep me waiting again. I don't think anyone in the front of the plane survived. I feel like my life is over, too." Her fiancé's name was Joseph Heartfelt.

From Joseph I. Frightened, 35, of Kansas City, MO: He was at the Delta Airlines ticket counter canceling his travel plans to fly to San Francisco. "Too many plane crashes. I just don't feel safe on a plane anymore."

From Enid R. Intrepid, 25, a University of Kansas graduate student in journalism: She was waiting for a flight to Seattle to visit her parents. "It was a terrible tragedy, but the law of averages is on the side of safety. I'm going ahead with my plans. Hundreds of people die in traffic accidents, but you still get in a car. You can't let these things frighten you. This was a freak accident. The storm is over and the sun is shining. I just know I'll be safe when I fly."

98

From Sam Adams, 23, a computer technician from Kansas City, MO: He was driving past the airport on his way home. "I saw this big orange flash in the sky. I wondered if that was the sun coming out after the storm. It was so bright. Then I saw the horrible flames and smoke and heard what happened on the radio."

From a spokesperson at St. Luke's Hospital: "We've been told to expect 30 victims. We can't handle any more. All personnel have been called in, and our emergency room is full. We can't release any names at this time."

From a spokesperson at the Kansas University Medical Center: "We have five of the survivors in our intensive-care burn unit. Fortunately we have the best facility in the state, and we're doing all we can. We are expecting more injured people momentarily."

21-2. Airplane crash – Day Two – Print Story

This is the second-day story of the plane crash. This is a deadline assignment. You have about an hour. Use whatever human-interest material you need for the mainbar. You do not have to use all of this material.

Many of the facts have changed, including the number of dead and injured. You have received a passenger list so you now have the names of those who died and those who survived, but the list will be published separately so don't worry about including it in your story. You are contacting relatives for some of your information – there will be separate sidebars on them – and officials of the airline, the airport, the National Transportation Safety Board, hospitals and so on. Not all the dead have been identified. You have contacted some relatives, and you will be at the airport to meet others who are arriving on two flights. Delta Airlines has flown in the relatives free of charge. One plane, Flight 222, is coming from Dallas; another, Flight 333, is arriving at 10 a.m. from New York.

Rescue workers worked throughout the night to clear the last of the bodies from the plane and the area. The wreckage of the plane is still on the edge of the runway. Investigators from the NTSB are still combing the wreckage. Although this concourse remains closed, the airport is open and planes are taking off on schedule at other concourses.

Delta Airlines spokesman I.M. Devastated says the death toll was higher than originally expected. The total death toll at this point is 234, with 50 survivors. Devastated says it is possible that some infants who were not on the passenger list might also have died, raising the death toll, but he is not certain at this time.

Included in the death toll are the pilot and two co-pilots and five of the six flight attendants. Also, five people who originally survived have died overnight in area hospitals. All but five of the remaining survivors are in the hospital. The five others were released last night.

Most of the injured have broken bones and 15 of them have severe burns. The burn victims are at the University of Kansas Medical Center. The others are at Liberty Hospital and St. Luke's Hospital.

The following information comes from other reporters but you may use it in your mainbar:

From Elsa M. Nurse, spokeswoman for KU Medical Center: She said she has never seen such extensive burns in all her 33 years at the hospital. "It's a wonder they survived at all," she said. "All the burn victims are in shock."

From St. Luke's Hospital: Every doctor and nurse has worked double shifts. The emergency room is filled with at least 40 area residents who are donating blood. "It's the least I can do," said Steve Marcus, 19, a University of Kansas sophomore. "We were lucky. My brother, Bob, was on that plane and he survived. He's here with a broken leg, a broken collar bone and a concussion, but at least he's alive." Marcus and his brother live at 2330 New Hampshire St. in Lawrence. Bob is 21, a senior majoring in journalism at KU. Bob Marcus is one of three survivors from Lawrence. Forty-five of the people who died also were from Lawrence.

From survivor Annie Grace Lucky, 47, a Dallas resident: She had flown to Missouri to visit a friend in Kansas City. She was one of the five released from the hospital. She was at the airport arranging with authorities to provide her limousine transportation to Dallas. This was her first plane trip. "I had always had a fear of flying," Lucky said. "I figured at my age, it was time to get over it. Now I'm afraid I won't. I'll never fly again. I expect this airline to get me home on the ground."

From survivor John Microchip, computer salesman: He works for Bigstate Computers in Dallas, corporate headquarters for his firm. He came to Kansas City for a business conference. He is in St. Luke's with a broken leg, a broken neck, several ruptured vertebrae and a broken arm. He said he saw the thunderclouds around the jet as it circled the airport, but he wasn't concerned at first. When the passengers behind him cried out in alarm at the turbulence, he said he told them, "Don't worry about it. It's just a typical thunderstorm. We're going to be safe." Then he added: "Suddenly it felt as though somebody stepped on us. The plane kind of rocked, and people began screaming and yelling. Nobody was expecting it. I saw the ground coming up. Then we hit. The plane bounced once. Then it bounced again. I opened my eyes, and there I was dangling 30 feet above the grass, still strapped into my seat belt. I thought that I had either arrived in heaven or on earth. Then I unbuckled my seat belt and fell to the ground."

From Janet Sorrow of Dallas: She lost her whole family. She arrived from Dallas on the morning flight. She was sobbing as she was escorted by airline personnel to the Delta Airlines hospitality suite where officials were waiting for her. Airline officials tried to stop reporters from talking to her, but she said before she went in that her husband, Bob, and her three children – Janet, 2, Robert Jr., 3, and Amy, 6 – were coming to Kansas City to start a new life. Bob was a carpenter and there wasn't any work in Dallas because of the oil recession, so he finally got a job in Kansas City after nine months of unemployment in Texas. "We were so happy at getting a new chance. I stayed behind and planned to join them in a few weeks because I had to handle the final details of selling our house. Now I have no home, no husband, no family. I wish I had died with them." *(continued)*

From Jennifer Agony of Dallas: She is 25, wife of crash victim, James L. Agony. She said her husband was taking a long weekend to visit friends in Kansas City. "Two months ago he got bumped from another Delta Airlines flight and was given a free ticket for another round trip. They told him he could fly anywhere, anytime he wanted to. He made the wrong choice," she said, sobbing.

From NTSB investigators: They said they are not sure yet, but they blame the crash on weather conditions. The winds were between 60 and 65 mph at the time the plane crashed, and lightning was in the area. Retired Coast Guard Adm. Patrick Bursely, the lead NTSB investigator, said it appears the plane might have hit a microburst. That is an upward air current surrounding a center of downward winds. It's known as wind shear and it will force a plane to plummet, he explains. It's a dangerous weather phenomenon.

Bursley seemed very upset. He said there is a question whether the pilot had received the most up-to-date weather forecast before he attempted his landing. Bursley said the black box has been recovered. He said: "There is indication of a weather forecast being delivered to controllers some 10 minutes before the accident, and that was not passed along to the pilot. It appears that both controllers involved and the pilots involved in this accident were not concerned about the immediate weather conditions."

He said controllers were advised about 15 minutes before the crash that cumulonimbus clouds had formed east of the airport. Such clouds are often associated with thunderstorms, which could contain violent wind shears. The latest weather forecast the pilot received before the crash was an hour old, he said. He added that he is basing all that information from the recording in the black box, which was recovered last night.

The National Weather Service reported that at the time the plane was making its final approach, a huge thunderstorm was 5,000 feet above the airport and was unleashing winds and lightning. The storm only arose over the airport area about 30 minutes before the plane crashed. Bursely said the pilot never got that information. The plane was in a landing pattern at 2,000 to 3,000 feet at that time.

From Kansas City Medical Examiner, Dr. Richard C. Froede: He is in charge of death certificates for all the victims. He said that determining the identity of all the dead could take days. He said so far, about 215 of the dead have been identified, but he is waiting for dental records to confirm the identification of the others.   "There are fragments of bodies that have been recovered. This was a gruesome crash. We may get to the point where some bodies may never be identified. I'm amazed anyone survived."

21-3. Airplane crash – Day Two – broadcast version

Use the same information to write a story of 1:45 for the evening news. You should use two sound bites and a standup. Following is the other video you have:

- Close-up, medium and wide shots of the wreckage
- Medium and wide shots of investigators going through the wreckage
- Medium shots of victims' families crying
- Medium and wide shots of the exteriors of the hospitals where victims were taken

21-4. Explosion

This is the kind of explosion that can happen in any community. Write a main story. You also should evaluate whether some of the material should not be used for ethical reasons. Write this two ways: a brief version that you will file immediately for the Web and a more complete version for the next day's newspaper. If your instructor prefers, write the full version for broadcast.

You are a reporter for *The Sun,* a daily newspaper in San Bernardino, Calif. It is shortly after 8 a.m. You are listening to the police radio and you hear a report that there has been an explosion. You call the police dispatcher and learn that a gasoline pipeline exploded in the same neighborhood in which a 69-car runaway freight train derailed about two weeks ago, either an ironic or relevant coincidence. When the freight train derailed, it crashed into a string of homes and killed two crew members in the train and two boys in one home. Police spokesman Gary Fahnestrock tells you:

"There has been an explosion. We haven't sorted anything out yet." Your editor tells you to get to the scene. You get to the scene where confusion reigns. You gather as much information as you can and return to the newspaper to write this story on deadline. You have about 45 minutes until deadline. You have gathered the information that follows for a location map. Here are your notes for the story:

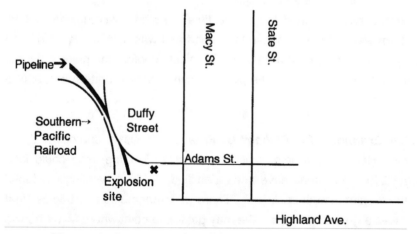

The explosion occurred at 8:11 a.m. in the neighborhood bounded by Duffy Street and Highland Ave., exactly the same area where the freight train derailed two weeks ago. When you arrive at Duffy Street, you see flames shooting about 100 feet into the air and seven homes on fire. You try to talk to as many people as possible. Here are your sources:

David Andries, an official of the Calnev gas company: He says the explosion was caused by a 14-inch gasoline pipeline that ruptured. The pipeline, which is buried six feet underground, carries unleaded fuel from Colton (a neighboring community) to Nevada. He says it sprayed fuel on the houses when it ruptured. "We don't know the cause of the break. It could have been the train, obviously," he says.

Gregory Garcia, a spokesman for the mayor of San Bernardino: About 700 people have been evacuated to the Red Cross evacuation center. The center has been set up at the Job Corps Center, 3753 Kerry St.

Theresa Schorder, a Red Cross worker: By 10 a.m. 30 residents from Duffy and Donald streets neighborhoods arrived at the center. Two vans and a bus are being used for the evacuation.

Paul Allaire, San Bernardino Fire Department spokesman: Two people have died in a home on Duffy Street. One body was burned beyond recognition. The other victim is believed to be a man. Firefighters are looking for a third victim in the home.

San Bernardino Councilwoman Valerie Pope-Ludlam who was at the scene: "A woman ran out of her house, she left behind her sister and her cousin and a 6-month-old baby inside, and she looked back and the house blew up behind her."

Phil Arviso, a council aide: He said he talked to the woman whom Pope-Ludlam mentioned. He said she was Robbie Brown of 2327 Duffy St. He said Brown said her relatives, Keesha Jefferson, Charlene Jefferson and Charlene's baby were in the house. "She actually said her house blew up behind her as she came out. The house is gone. If anybody was in there, they went with it."

Bill Stewart, an insurance agent who was visiting a client, Martha Franklin in a house in the 2300 block of Donald Street, which borders Adams Street (about a block away from the explosion): "We were sitting at the table and we heard this loud noise, and it just started getting bigger. I ran to the window and looked out and could see nothing but smoke; then we both hit the floor. We waited for it to blow over, but it didn't go away. Then we started to head for the door and when she opened the door, the smoke just started rolling in. We looked outside. The grass was burning – green grass burning. Everything was burning, even the concrete."

Calnev pipeline General Manager Jed Robinson: He said the pipeline can carry more than 3.3 million gallons of fuel, jet fuel, gasoline and diesel – which flows through the 14-inch pipeline daily. The pipeline was carrying unleaded gasoline. He said valves along the pipe fall into place whenever anything in the pipe starts to flow backward, toward Colton where the pipeline starts. He said a valve near the fire may not be completely closed, and that could influence the time it takes to put out the fire. "With that kind of a volatile fuel, you have to use some sort of foam. Normally where there is not an awful lot of fuel, you just contain it and try and let it burn out." He said he didn't know how much fuel is in the pipe.

Miretta Brumlow, a resident of 2351 Adams St. near the site: She was at the first aid center set up at Macy Street. She was still wearing a nightgown. "I felt my whole house shake. I thought it was an earthquake. Then I looked out and I saw the fire and I just started crying. I ran to the bedroom and got my daughter and grandson out, then I started looking for my pets, and

103

then I just had to get out. I think my cats are still in there. Everything I own was in that house." She said she is a student at San Bernardino Valley College, but she hasn't attended school since the railroad disaster because she's been afraid to leave her children at home. "Thank God I didn't go to my class at eight o'clock this morning."

San Bernardino City Attorney Jim Penman, who toured the area this morning from a helicopter: "We were assured by the pipeline people it was safe (after the railroad accident) and the experts who examined it said there was no danger."

From hospital officials: Seven burn victims were admitted to the San Bernardino County Medical Center. Their conditions were not available. Other people admitted and treated were: Tina Blackburn, who is in serious condition with second- and third-degree burns over 15 percent of her body; Michael Howard with burns on his hands; his wife, Janet Howard, with third-degree burns and their two children, Shirley, 1, and LaKedra, 2, who were being treated for smoke inhalation. Diane Tucker was treated for minor cuts.

Observations and general information you receive from various sources: Southern California Gas Co. workers were in the neighborhood to shut off gas lines to avoid any possibility of natural gas explosion, they said. A thick cloud of gray-black smoke from the explosion was reported visible as far away as Riverside and Ontario (neighboring communities). Highland Avenue at Macy was closed to motorists.

You are out of time. You must return to the newspaper and write the story. Use today as your time frame. This story will be in print in about 90 minutes.

Based on a story from *The* (San Bernardino, Calif.,) *Sun,* Used with permission.

21-5. Basic weather feature

Write a feature story about the weather. First brainstorm several angles you might take if you are having a hot, cold, dry, wet or other unusual stretch of weather. Interview students and other people on campus about how they are reacting to the weather. Is business in your area affected by the weather? Interview some business people, city or campus officials about costs they might be incurring because of the weather. Make sure you get human-interest angles. Check the forecast for your area and record high and low temperatures for the month or day by accessing any weather sites or going to *http://www.weather.com*.

Media Jobs and Internships

22

22-1. Internet job search

You want to find out what jobs are available in your field. Your textbook mentions job searching opportunities available on the Internet and it lists several sites on the CourseMate at *http://www.cengagebrain.com*. Find at least five sites that offer information about job opportunities of interest to you in your field. List the name of the sites and the Internet addresses that you find most helpful.

    a.

    b.

    c.

    d.

    e.

22-2. Research the organization

Before you decide where to apply for a job or internship, you should conduct research about the kinds of opportunities that are available and about the organization to which you wish to apply. Most organizations have sites on the Web, so be sure to check for them and research the organization before you apply. But never rely on directories to be up to date with names of people. Always call to find out to whom you should send your resume.

    List at least three organizations in which you would be interested for an internship or a job. Write the name and address of the person to whom you should send your resume, and include any other information required for a job application with this organization.

    a.

    b.

    c.

22-3. Social Media for Job or Internship Research

Check the social media links of at least three organizations where you might like to have an internship.

1. Write a brief explanation of the company's presence (or not) on these social media sites:
   a. Facebook

   b. Twitter

   c. YouTube

   d. Other?

2. List the names of three people who are influential in the careers or companies you where would like to work. Find them on LinkedIn and write a brief explanation of their bios.

   a.

   b.

   c.

3. List three people, companies or organizations you would like to follow for your career or job search on Twitter or Facebook and find their sites:

   a.

   b.

   c.

Appendix Grammar and Usage

Exercise 1. Active/passive and it's/its

Active/Passive: Identify whether active or passive voice is used in the following sentences by circling the correct item:

1. John Smith was nominated for fraternity president by Joe Chance.

     a. Active
     b. Passive

2. Judge Raymond Burr sentenced the man convicted of driving under the influence of alcohol to two years in jail.

     a. Active
     b. Passive

3. Students conducted a rally yesterday to raise money.
     a. Active
     b. Passive

4. The case was dismissed by a three-judge panel.

     a. Active
     b. Passive

Choose which sentence uses the correct form of its or it's.

5.   a. Its important for you to learn the difference between these two words.
       b. It's important for you to learn the difference between these two words.

6.   a. The dog chased its tail for hours.
       b. The dog chased it's tail for hours.

7.   a. When its time for you to graduate, you need to fill out several forms.
       b. When it's time for you to graduate, you need to fill out several forms.

8. a. The university lost its accreditation last year.
    b. The university lost it' accreditation last year.

9. a. The newspaper won its first Pulitzer Prize this year.
    b. The newspaper won it's first Pulitzer Prize this year.

10. a. It's important for you to use proper grammar in your e-mail.
    b. Its important for you to use proper grammar in your e-mail.

Exercise 2. That/Which and Who/Whom

Choose the correct version of the following sentences:

1. a. The student production of *Macbeth*, which is the third play the drama club is planning this year, will be in March.
    b. The student production of *Macbeth* that is the third play the drama club is planning this year will be in March.

2. a. This is the test that you must take on Monday.
    b. This is the test, which you must take, on Monday.

3. a. Alaska, which is the 49th state, is one of the most beautiful states in the nation.
    b. Alaska that is the 49th state is one of the most beautiful states in the nation.

4. a. The University of Kansas basketball team, which had many freshmen players this year, made it to the Final Four.
    b. The University of Kansas basketball team that had many freshmen players this year made it to the Final Four.

5. a. The computer lab, which contains the Macintosh computers, was vandalized.
    b. The computer lab that contains the Macintosh computers was vandalized.

The following sentences test your knowledge of who or whom:

6. a. The person who is in charge of hiring is the one whom you should contact.
    b. The person whom is in charge of hiring is the one who you should contact.

7. a. Who do you plan to see when you go for your job interview?
    b. Whom do you plan to see when you go for your job interview?

8. a. These are the officials who will make the decision about whether your organization gets the money.

b. These are the officials whom will make the decision about whether your organization gets the money.

9. a. Do you know who is in charge of the event?

b. Do you know whom is in charge of the event?

10. a. I don't know who was responsible but whoever stole the fraternity mascot will be caught.

b. I don't know whom was responsible but whomever stole the fraternity mascot will be caught.

Exercise 3. Action verbs vs. linking verbs (essay format)

Rewrite these sentences using action verbs. Verbs that express action are preferable to linking verbs (is, are, was, were) that simply link a subject to a noun or pronoun. Whenever you start a sentence with *there*, an expletive, you are forced to use a weak linking verb. For example:

Weak: There *were* 13 students who marched in the parade.
Stronger action verb: Thirteen students *marched* in the parade.

1. There was in increase in tuition last year in universities throughout the nation.

2. There are rising costs for employee benefits that contributed to the increased tuition.

3. There is new legislation that would reduce interest rates on federally backed student loans.

4. There are many students who need to improve their grammar skills before they can become good writers.

5. There were 17 students who attended the lecture, but there were many others who decided to stay home because of the inclement weather.

Exercise 4. Dangling modifiers (essay format)

Rewrite the following sentences to correct the dangling modifiers:

a. Carrying his books in his backpack, the strap broke.

b. When planning a meeting, an agenda is advisable.

c. While discussing the election, the topic of privacy and politicians aroused heated debate.

d. Living in a small town for many years, the large population of this city overwhelmed him.

Exercise 5. Run-on sentences (essay format)

When two complete sentences are joined by a comma, they are called "run-on" sentences or "comma splices." Use a period or a semicolon if the two sentences are very closely related in thought. A period is always a safe choice. You may also use conjunctions such as *and, but, or, for, nor* preceded by a comma. Determine whether these sentences are run-on sentences or are correct. Fix them if they are incorrect.

a. You may pay your tuition with a credit card, it's a new university policy.

b. Many states are trying to pass legislation to make English the only permissible language for government business, a policy that several Spanish-speaking groups oppose.

c. The election was highly contested, the candidates were glad when it was over.

d. A fire during a Halloween dance was one of the deadliest fires in Sweden, at least 62 people were killed.

e. More than 60 people were killed, 173 others were injured, when flames erupted in the dance hall filled with teenagers.

Exercise 6. General Usage

Test your knowledge of usage covered in your textbook. Choose the correct item:

1.   a. The media are often blamed for poor coverage of politics.
          b. The media is often blamed for poor coverage of politics.

2.   a. The student felt bad after she took the test.
          b. The student felt badly after she took the test.

110

3.   a. I am anxious to get a new job.
      b. I am eager to get a new job.

4.   a. He thought it was alright to turn his paper in a few days late.
      b. He thought it was all right to turn his paper in a few days late.

5.   a. The Board of Education met last night, and they plan to resume discussion of the
      proposal next week.
      b. The Board of Education met last night, and it plans to resume discussion of the proposal
      next week.

6.   a. Some people thought the president's behavior was embarassing.
      b. Some people thought the president's behavior was embarrassing.

7.   a. Each of the board members know what they must do.
      b. Each of the board members knows what he must do.

8.   a. How much farther do we have to go before we reach the lake?
      b. How much further do we have to go before we reach the lake?

9.   a. If I were in your position, I would quit.
      b. a. If I was in your position, I would quit.

10.   a. None of the women in the class was planning to go on to graduate school.
      b. None of the women in the class were planning to go on to graduate school.

11.   a. It's clear that the argument was between he and his wife.
      b. It's clear that the argument was between him and his wife.

12.   a. The date for submitting the advertising campaign was not going to work out for either he
      or his boss.
      b. The date for submitting the advertising campaign was not going to work out for either him
      or his boss.

13.   a. Give the free pizza to whomever shows up first.
      b. Give the free pizza to whoever shows up first.

14.   a. Do you know who hit the most home runs?
      b. Do you know whom hit the most home runs?

15.   a. You never know who you will run into when you go to the cafe.
      b. You never know whom you will run into when you go to the cafe.

16.   a. I know I laid the book on the table last night, but it disappeared.
        b. I know I lay the book on the table last night, but it disappeared.

17.   a. You should have used better judgement.
        b. You should have used better judgment.

18.   a. The journalism school, which is on K Street, is the building with the green roof.
        b. The journalism school that is on K Street is the building with the green roof.

19.   a. If you lose the election, you can run again next semester.
        b. If you loose the election, you can run again next semester.

20.   a. If I was in a better mood, I'd let you skip this test.
        b. a. If I were in a better mood, I'd let you skip this test.

21.   a. Less than five students showed up for the presentation.
        b. Fewer than five students showed up for the presentation.

22.   a. The disagreement is strictly between you and I.
        b. The disagreement is strictly between you and me.

23.   a. If you studied a lot of these items in your textbook, you should do well.
        b. If you studied alot of these items in your textbook, you should do well.

24.   a. Either the professor or the graduate assistant is going to bring the test.
        b. Either the professor or the graduate assistant are going to bring the test.

25.   a. Each of the students expects to get an A.
        b. Each of the students expect to get an A.